MW00443443

Nowhere to Remember

Hanford Histories

Volume I

Michael Mays, Series Editor

Nowhere to Remember

Hanford, White Bluffs, and Richland to 1943

Edited by
Robert Bauman and Robert Franklin

WSU
PRESS

Washington State University Press
Pullman, Washington

Washington State University Press
PO Box 645910
Pullman, Washington 99164-5910
Phone: 800-354-7360
Fax: 509-335-8568
Email: wsupress@wsu.edu
Website: wsupress.wsu.edu

© 2018 by the Board of Regents of Washington State University
All rights reserved
First printing 2018

Printed and bound in the United States of America on pH neutral, acid-free paper. Reproduction or transmission of material contained in this publication in excess of that permitted by copyright law is prohibited without permission in writing from the publisher.

Library of Congress Cataloging-in-Publication Data

Names: Bauman, Robert, 1964- editor of compilation. | Franklin, Robert, 1981- editor of compilation.
Title: Nowhere to remember : Hanford, White Bluffs, and Richland to 1943 / edited by Robert Bauman and Robert Franklin.
Other titles: Hanford, White Bluffs, and Richland to 1943
Description: Pullman, Washington : Washington State University Press, [2018] | Series: Hanford histories ; volume 1 | Includes bibliographical references and index.
Identifiers: LCCN 2018015309 | ISBN 9780874223606 (alk. paper)
Subjects: LCSH: Hanford (Wash.)--History. | White Bluffs (Wash.)--History. | Richland (Wash.)--History. | World War, 1939-1945--Evacuation of civilians--Washington (State)--Benton County. | Internally displaced persons--Washington (State)--Benton County. | Farm life--Washington (State)--Benton County. | Interviews--Washington (State)--Benton County. | Benton County (Wash.)--Biography. | Memory--Social aspects--Washington (State)--Columbia River Valley. | Hanford Site (Wash.)--History.
Classification: LCC F899.H36 N69 2018 | DDC 979.7/51--dc23 LC record available at https://lccn.loc.gov/2018015309

On the cover: Hanford High School, 2018. *National Park Service.*

Contents

Illustrations

Acknowledgments

This volume and the series of which it is a part would not have been possible without the support and contributions of a number of individuals and institutions. This series of volumes originated with the Hanford Oral History Project, begun in 2013. That project was created with the support of the Hanford History Partnership. We would like to express our sincere appreciation to the members of that partnership, particularly Ron Kathren of the Herbert M. Parker Foundation, Colleen French of the Department of Energy, Gary Petersen of TRIDEC, Maynard Plahuta of the B Reactor Museum Association, Vanessa Moore and the late CJ Mitchell of the African American Community Cultural and Educational Society (AACCES), and Ann Roseberry from the Richland Public Library. The Oral History Project and this volume would not have happened without their generosity, support, and guidance.

A special thanks to Sarah St. Hilaire for her extraordinary research assistance for the first year of the Oral History Project. Sarah provided brilliant background research on each of the early interviewees and their families which greatly benefited the project. Also, a special thanks to Anneke Rachinski who coordinated the Oral History Project and scheduled most of the interviews in 2013 and 2014. Anneke and Sarah both brought an exceptional energy and enthusiasm to the project that was missed once they moved on to other opportunities. In addition, Morgan Flaherty provided excellent research support during her brief time working on the project. Neither the project nor this volume would have happened without the efforts of Sarah, Anneke, and Morgan.

Thank you to our friends and colleagues at Pacific Northwest Television and Northwest Public Radio—particularly Tom Hungate, Linda Pasch, and Greg Mills—who recorded all of these interviews for us. Their professionalism and cooperation have been a tremendous benefit to the project.

The Hanford History Project, encompassing the Hanford Oral History Project as well as documents and artifacts from the Department of Energy's Hanford Operations Office, was founded in 2014. Since then, a number of students have provided important research that has benefited the production of this volume. Those students include David Boling-broke, Emma Rice, Elinor Lake, Catalina Le, Adrian Holgate, Mauren Jones, and Amanda Pearson. Without the efforts and support of Jillian Gardner-Andrews, who took over the scheduling of oral histories in 2017 and participates in every Hanford History Project outreach event, we could not have completed the work.

A special thank you to the oral history transcriptionist, Evelyn Moos, who has watched and re-watched every Hanford Oral History Project video to create and edit the transcripts used in the publication of this book. Transcription is a time-intensive task, often taking three to five times the length of the interview. Evelyn's attention to detail and knowledge of Hanford history has been an invaluable asset to the Hanford History Project. The oral histories, with full transcripts, can be found online at www.hanfordhistory.com.

Stephanie Button at the East Benton County Historical Society and Museum provided research assistance and photographs used in the making of this volume. Stephanie threw open the EBCHSM archives to us on numerous occasions and her support is greatly appreciated.

Bob Clark at WSU Press has believed in this project from the beginning and enthusiastically advocated for it. Indeed, this volume and the series of which it is a part, would not have happened without Bob. All of us involved with this volume would like to thank him for his unending support. Also, special thanks to the WSU Press staff Ed Sala, Caryn Lawton, Beth DeWeese, and Kerry Darnall; and to the WSU Press Editorial Board for their belief in our efforts. To Mike Mays, the series editor for this volume and those to follow, our thanks for your unwavering support.

The authors and co-editors have presented versions of the material in this volume at a few different academic conferences. We would like to thank commenters and audience members at the Pacific Northwest History Conference (both 2014 in Vancouver and 2017 in Spokane), the Oral History Association Conference in Tampa, Florida, in 2015, and the Western History Association Conference in San Diego in 2017. Questions and comments at those gatherings have made this volume richer and fuller.

The co-editors would like to especially thank our friends and family members who have provided so much support and inspiration over the past couple of years. Bob Bauman would like to offer special gratitude to Stephanie, Robert, and Rachel Bauman; and, Robert Franklin, again, to Evelyn Moos. And, of course, props to our co-authors, Laura Arata and Dave Harvey, whose contributions go well beyond their expertise and excellent chapters in this volume. Here's to terrific colleagues and friends, as well as fellow conference panel members and historians!

Finally, we would like to thank all of the individuals whose interviews provided much of the background for the content of this volume. Their stories demonstrate the importance of oral history and preserving the memory of places like Hanford and White Bluffs. It is to those former residents that we dedicate this book.

Abbreviations

The following abbreviations for manuscript collections and newspapers are used throughout the notes.

EBCHSM	East Benton County Historical Society and Museum
HCRL	Hanford Cultural Resources Laboratory Oral History Program
HHP	Hanford History Project

Preface

From 1943 on, the Hanford, Washington, region—with its Manhattan Project ties and its massive nuclear reservation—has been known (if known at all) primarily as a secretive, destructive, and highly contaminated federal enclave, a long-standing site of controversy and, often, of infamy and shame. Yet an overly narrow focus on Hanford's role in the war effort or, conversely, the monumental cleanup effort now underway, masks the complexities and contradictions of an isolated provincial site that, despite its remoteness, embodies many of the most pressing geopolitical issues of the entire span of the twentieth century and beyond. Indeed, the area already had a rich and complicated—if now largely forgotten—set of interwoven histories well before 1943.

These histories begin some 12,000 years ago with the last of the Ice Age Floods, then vault ahead to encompass the migration stories of indigenous Native American and pioneering European settler communities; continue through Hanford's role in the Manhattan Project and Cold War; and bring us more recently to its ongoing role in delivering cutting-edge science and engineering in the areas of human health, waste remediation, and environmental sciences. Over the last century, those histories have cut across radically diverse areas of academic and historical inquiry including, for instance, the military-industrial complex, the Second World War, the history of science, the rise of agribusiness, the sociology and politics of the Cold War, the impact of hydropower on natural and human habitats, segregation and civil rights, literatures of the environment, and the impact of technology on the American West. The list could go on and on.

Nowhere to Remember: Hanford, White Bluffs, and Richland to 1943 is the first volume in the Washington State University Press Hanford Histories series. Upcoming volumes will focus on science and the environment, race and diversity, constructing Hanford, the Manhattan Project and its legacies, and an illustrated history of Hanford. The series stems from a partnership between the press and WSU Tri-Cities' Hanford History Project and grew out of a shared perception regarding both the broad range of stories that make up Hanford's unique history and the relative lack of existing research on that history. We agree that while there are countless stories to be told, to date very few of them have been.

While not necessarily intentional, it is nevertheless appropriate that the first volume in the series should focus on the pre-Manhattan Project period and those communities the federal government's atomic program displaced. The Hanford History Project (HHP) was established in 2014 to foster greater understanding and awareness of the vital role the Mid-Columbia region of Washington State—both its people and its environment—has played on the national and international stage. Collaborative from the start, HHP's first initiative was the development of an oral history program that would complement, supplement, and coordinate existing oral history efforts in the community, some of which date back two decades or more. With seed funding provided by the United States Department of Energy (DOE), HHP's initial focus was on capturing the stories of the rapidly declining pool of residents who inhabited White Bluffs, Hanford, and Richland Village before 1943. The history of these communities from their origins in the late nineteenth century up until the middle of World War II was altogether typical of many other nascent agricultural communities throughout the western United States. There existed a shared experience of the arrival of irrigation, a dependence on railroads, and common struggles and survival during the Great Depression. Little could the residents of these communities imagine how radically their fates would diverge from their fellow frontiersmen with the arrival of government troops in 1943. *Nowhere to Remember* leans heavily on the oral histories that HHP and others have recorded over the years to recount a history that would otherwise very likely have vanished along with those displaced communities.

Since its inception, the oral history program has grown to include some 170 new personal narratives ranging from early Hanford and Cold War workers to the wives and children of Hanford employees whose lives were shaped by a culture of secrecy, those involved in cleanup, and most recently, African Americans whose lives were impacted in one way or another by the Hanford Site. It has also digitized and transcribed the oral history collections of partner community groups such as the African American Community Cultural and Educational Society, the B Reactor Museum Association, and the Herbert M. Parker Foundation.

Having begun with capturing oral histories, HHP has greatly expanded its scope over the last several years in a variety of ways: through its partnerships and collaborations with like-minded local, regional, and national organizations; through the development of multidisciplinary Hanford-based curricula; through educational outreach activities; through the collection, storage, and preservation of public and private artifacts, and archival and photographic collections; and through its housing and management of the Department of Energy's Hanford Collection, an assemblage of several thousand Hanford Site artifacts and archives collected over more than twenty years and dating from the beginning of the Manhattan Project at Hanford (1943) through the end of the Cold War (1990).

The artifacts in the Hanford Collection are extensive and many of them have important things to tell us about evolving innovations in science and technology. But many more offer a different view of the story, from the recreational activities of the workers to glimpses into domestic life in Hanford Camp and later in Richland (and Pasco, where African-American laborers were required to live). Thus they also tell us a great deal about the segregation that defined working and living conditions at the camp and beyond. Racial segregation during the construction of the site was pronounced, with separate barracks, swimming holes, and mess halls for blacks and whites. But segregation was equally rife with regard to gender and labor classifications as well. The "Alphabet Houses" that populate Richland to this day are quaint. But they were also mechanisms of control and of social ordering. The Hanford Collection reminds us just how many stories there are remaining to be told.

The Hanford History Project's mission is two-fold: to facilitate and promote scholarly research that explores the forces and tensions that have shaped the region across a broad range of disciplines; and to foster and coordinate educational outreach efforts through a variety of community activities and events including lectures, seminars, conferences, workshops, and life-long learning opportunities. WSU Press is an indispensable partner in both respects.

Akin to the community's oral histories—which have been recorded on a myriad of media formats and stored in shoe boxes, closets, garages, and attics—the archival records pertaining to the Hanford Site are scattered across the region and throughout the country. As we continue to consolidate those existing materials in one central archive, house them according to the highest professional standards of archival practices, and make them widely available through both physical and electronic means, we expect to attract scholars conducting research across a vast range of academic interests including, as noted above, the environment, fish and wildlife, diplomacy and diplomatic history, technology, waste remediation, health physics, history of science, the Second World War, the rise of agribusiness, and countless other topics. Together, through the Hanford Histories series, HHP and WSU Press are endeavoring to bring together the fragments of this fractured history, to make visible and coherent the various threads of that history for current and future generations, and to provide a much-needed venue for future research, be it in the academic or the public sphere.

Hanford Histories was established, then, to encourage and support new research by those working in diverse fields but at the leading edge of a common subject—Hanford and its stories. We seek to identify and encourage research that broadens, extends, and diversifies traditional academic disciplines; that approaches familiar subjects in unfamiliar ways; and that, at its very best, inaugurates whole new fields of scholarly inquiry. We will strive to create a catalogue in which groundbreaking work of a more narrow scope (regardless of discipline or field of interest) sits comfortably aside high quality work with general appeal. In this spirit we invite and will actively seek out work that reflects these values.

It is time, finally—a lifetime now removed from the evictions of the residents of White Bluffs and Hanford and the inception of the Manhattan Project—to gather together these diverse histories as part of a wholesale reconsideration of the events both large and small that irrevocably changed the course of human history. That Hanford, chosen largely because of its remoteness and its isolation, should play such a central and prominent role in those events is a paradox worthy of a scholarly tome in its own right. Yet no single volume, nor even a series of volumes written over the next decade, will tell the full story of what unfolded here over the last three-quarters of a century and beyond. That record will take ages for the historians to sort out.

The desire to provide a comprehensive accounting for such a multidimensional swath of history, even one as limited in geographic scope as this, will likely be perceived by many as idealistic at best or, less charitably, as hopelessly naïve. Yet the Hanford Histories series is, if nothing else, ambitious—as befits its subject. Moreover, there are good reasons to believe the time is ripe to launch such an ambitious project. From its beginning, secrecy prevailed at the processing facilities. Most workers were privy only to the operations of their highly segregated assignments. Security remained stringent during the ensuing years of the Cold War. Nor did a revamped mission do much to change things. Turning from production to cleanup, the site remained as secure, and as secretive, as ever. Through the decades, the archival and artifactual vestiges of our history—those once-upon-a-time cutting-edge technologies which suffered the inevitable indignity of obsolescence as they succumbed to ever more advanced technologies—remained locked away, sequestered behind the gates of one of the securest places in the country, out of sight and largely out of mind. But as the Cold War waned, and following the signing of the Tri-Party Agreement which created a comprehensive cleanup and compliance plan for the site in 1989, the shroud of secrecy began to lift. As records trickled out and as information began to become available, details of that clandestine history have emerged. While much of the story remains classified, the hard work of historical understanding has been underway for some time. Most importantly, the effort to tell the story of the Manhattan Project and Cold War received a tremendous boost when Congress enacted legislation at the end of 2014 creating the Manhattan Project National Historical Park (MAPR). That park is unique within the National Park System (NPS) because it is both co-managed by the U.S. Departments of Interior and Energy and co-located at the three primary Manhattan Project sites (Hanford, Washington; Los Alamos, New Mexico; and Oak Ridge, Tennessee). Its charge is "to preserve, interpret, and facilitate access to key historic resources associated with the Manhattan Project" (www.nps.gov/mapr/foundation-document.htm). As our nation's official storyteller, the Park Service, through MAPR, will provide the history of the people, events, science, and engineering that led to the creation of the atomic bomb. While not solely focused on the Manhattan Project, the Hanford Histories series seeks to complement the park in its interpretive mission in order to foster a better understanding of the profound historical lessons the nuclear program has to teach us—lessons about the grandeur of human ingenuity and perseverance on one hand and the calamity of human fallibility on the other.

All of us who are committed to the preservation and greater understanding of Hanford's remarkable history owe a debt of gratitude to Washington State University Press: its editor-in-chief, Robert A. Clark; its director, Edward Sala; its editorial board; and its staff. In their vision and foresight they have recognized not only the significant value of this history but also, especially, the urgency in capturing and preserving the first-hand accounts of the witnesses to these events before they are lost altogether in the passage of time.

Michael Mays
Director, Hanford History Project
Washington State University Tri-Cities

"Making a History of It May Help"

The Hanford Site and Its Spaces and Places of Meaning

Robert Franklin and Robert Bauman

When asked to explain why he thought conducting oral histories of former residents of the town of White Bluffs was important, Dick Wiehl, one of the first former residents of the Priest Rapids Valley interviewed by the Hanford Oral History Project, replied, "a town once started should live out its natural life, and this did not happen with White Bluffs. Its natural life was truncated suddenly by presidential decree. I think an effort should be made to still let White Bluffs live out its natural life. Making a history of it may help."[1] This volume uses the voices of the former residents, like Wiehl, of White Bluffs, Hanford, and Richland, in part to help those communities live out their natural lives.

Located in southeastern Washington State, the Hanford region was home to Native peoples, particularly the Wanapum, for thousands of years and to white settlers for about fifty years. But for the past seventy-five years, the site has been occupied by the Hanford Nuclear Reservation, location of the first production nuclear reactor in the United States, and also most of the nuclear waste in the United States. As a result, the Hanford Site is a place with a contested and conflicted past. Both popular memory and scholarship on Hanford have reflected that controversy. The study and memory of Hanford's role in the Atomic West revolves around two primary politically-charged narratives: Hanford as part of America's triumphal World War II and Cold War efforts; or Hanford as a place of environmental waste and danger.

This binary narrative has evolved in key scholarship on Hanford. Important works, such as Richard Rhodes' *The Making of the Atomic Bomb*, Michele Gerber's *On the Home Front*, and Michael D'Antonio's *Atomic Harvest*, written in the 1980s and 1990s, emphasized one or the other of those two primary narratives. A more recent and celebrated work on Hanford, Kate Brown's *Plutopia*, while telling a much more complicated story of Hanford by comparing it to a similar site, Ozersk, in Russia, still presents Hanford as a dangerous environmental wasteland. In much of this scholarship, the people involved in the development of Hanford are largely ignored, portrayed as either heroes or patriots, or as victims of government duplicity and nuclear radiation and other related hazards.[2]

One of the few early scholars to tell a more complex story about Hanford was Patricia Nelson Limerick. In her essay, "The Significance of Hanford in American History," Limerick identified Hanford not as an outlier, but as fitting well within the central themes of New Western scholarship. In particular, Limerick noted that Hanford fit "the pattern of cyclical displacements" that are central to the American West. As Limerick observed, "when a nuclear reactor displaces an apple orchard, the symbolism becomes so heavy-handed that it seems like an invention of a clumsy novelist—except that it happens to be true." For Limerick, Hanford also fit into the boom-and-bust cycle of western history, and as a representative of that cycle, now contains an impressive collection of "ruins and relics of lost times," including Indian artifacts, nuclear reactors turned into museums, and the sidewalks and shells of a few buildings of the former towns of Hanford and White Bluffs.[3]

While Limerick began to expand the narratives of Hanford by connecting it to key western themes, some recent scholarship has continued to complicate those stories further and present a more nuanced interpretation of the Hanford region—in particular, the people who lived and worked there. Brian Freer's "Atomic Pioneers and Environmental Legacy at the Hanford Site" examines the social identities of Hanford workers in the first ten years of nuclear production. Robert Bauman's "Jim Crow in the Tri-Cities" presents the experiences of African Americans who migrated from the South to work at Hanford as well as the system of segregation constructed by the DuPont Company and various government agencies in response to that migration. John Findlay's and Bruce Hevly's seminal work on Hanford, *Atomic Frontier Days*, offers a picture that examines the interweaving of politics, culture, science, and environment at Hanford and in the Tri-Cities. And Lee Ann Powell's "Culture, Cold War, Conservatism and the End of the Atomic Age" explores the connections between Hanford, Cold War Richland, the anti-nuclear movement, and the growth of conservatism in the 1960s and 1970s. While these more recent studies of Hanford have greatly enriched our understanding of the region and some of its people, often lost in these narratives are the lives of the pre-1943 residents of the towns of Hanford, White Bluffs, and Richland. Native peoples lived on the land for thousands of years, and in the late nineteenth century white families began to settle the region. Both of these ethnic groups would lose their land to America's efforts in World War II and the Cold War.[4]

Before Hanford overshadowed the Priest Rapids Valley, the area was a small, but vibrant, rural agricultural area. The development of agriculture came later to the arid areas of the West, and the history of Hanford, White Bluffs, and Richland fits within a larger historiography of the arid West. Works on agricultural history often ignore the arid West as that discipline is firmly rooted in East, South, and Midwest agricultural systems. A convenient, if predictable, place to start is with the role of the Frontier Thesis in shaping American identity, through the work of Frederick Jackson Turner. Turner's signature 1893 work "The Significance of the Frontier in American History" and its contention that the western frontier shaped American identity is a foundation for American West scholarship and has influenced generations of scholars and citizens. The problems of Turner's thesis are many—it ignores gender and race, and relies on a simplistic dialectic between civilization and savagery to explain the creation of a unique American character. Turner glosses over the arid West, viewing farming as possible only in temperate, well-watered areas. Certainly the irrigated landscape of Washington's Columbia Basin falls outside the margins of Turner's western vision. The Frontier Thesis still serves as a bedrock cultural premise with which many residents of the arid West self-identify: individuality, ruggedness, and self-reliance—concepts that ignore the historical reality of massive government, military, and infrastructure spending that made settlement in the arid West possible.[5]

Walter Prescott Webb's classic *The Great Plains* was the next major work to tackle the West as a region of influence, and unlike Turner, Webb differentiated between the arid West and the more-humid Midwest. To Webb, the arid West required new forms of farming (irrigation) and new water laws in comparison to the East. The West is a hard region to generalize, however, and like Turner, Webb's analysis ignores issues of class, gender, and race in the West. These issues received better treatment by the "New Western Historians" such as Limerick and others noted below, who examined class, race, and gender within larger political and legal systems of water use and land settlement law.[6]

Regional history of the arid Pacific Northwest provides an opportunity to focus on the unique geographical features found in such a diverse climate. In *The Great Columbia Plain*, Donald Meinig combines a historical and geographical analysis of an overlooked area of the American West, the open country of interior Washington, Oregon, and Idaho that now makes up some of the most productive farmland in the nation. Meinig's work succeeds by balancing the attitudes toward the region, the geographical considerations and challenges, and the changing economic forces affecting the Columbia Basin. Although written half a century ago, it stands as an excellent analysis of nineteenth century Pacific Northwest history. Covering such a large area over an entire century, however, left Meinig little space to focus on the Priest Rapids Valley and its contribution and transition in the arid West.[7]

Other important works that relate to the history of the arid West include Mark Fiege's *Irrigated Eden*, Donald Worster's *Rivers of Empire*, Leah S. Glaser's *Electrifying the Rural American West*, and Lawrence Mac-Donnell's *From Reclamation to Sustainability*. In perhaps the best scholarly treatment of the history of the irrigated West, Fiege asks all of us to look hard at the language we use to describe the physical environment, and our distinction between "natural" and "unnatural" spaces. By examining the "ingenious, intricate, technological system" of irrigation works in the Snake River Plain of Idaho, Fiege notes the ability of nature to respond to human efforts, and the countervailing human effort to shape nature as a modification, not an erasure of "natural" spaces, of the pre-existing environment. Nature has agency in the irrigated and arid West, and this area is truly on the frontlines of a constant back-and-forth process of alteration and layering that has been playing out for thousands of years. Fiege illustrates well the hope and struggles of irrigators, the rosy and glowing advertisements describing the potential of arid lands to be unlocked by reliable water, and the resulting dance between nature and human effort that goes on in the West to this day. The farmers of Hanford and White Bluffs engaged in the same processes of transformation of their patch of the arid West, and were challenged by the natural world around them.[8]

Worster contends that the true West is "a culture and society built on, and absolutely dependent on, a sharply alienating, intensely managerial relationship with nature." Worster draws a sharp line between the beautiful and untrammeled vistas of the West and the irrigation works and reclaimed lands heavily molded by human hands—both of which are the West. Glaser finds the intersection between rural life and the benefits of industrialization, but rather than paint rural Americans as backward or victims of industrialization, she argues that rural communities maintain identity by incorporating technology on their own terms. MacDonnell turns his attention to the ability of irrigation water supply organizations, and the local people that create, support, and use them, to meet traditional water supply needs. Dichotomies of a different sort underlie MacDonnell's work—how does agriculture become the basis for settlement of a region with inadequate rainfall to grow crops? What factors drive agricultural development in the West, which is so vast and mountainous and yet the most urbanized region in the country? MacDonnell rightfully exposes the lack of scholarly attention on irrigated agriculture by "New Western-ers," which is puzzling because the development of the West is rooted in irrigated agriculture, and by agricultural historians who are still Midwest-, East-, and South-focused in their scholarship. Clearly there is more room for scholarly treatment of agriculture west of the breadbasket.[9]

This book hopes in part to fill that void by focusing on rural agricultural communities in the Priest Rapids Valley of eastern Washington. It is the first in a multi-volume series using oral histories to tell the story of the Hanford region. It focuses on the small towns of Hanford, White Bluffs, and Richland, three small agricultural communities in the Mid-Columbia region of eastern Washington in the years before World War II.

In many ways these towns were typical agricultural communities in the American West, relying on irrigation for their crops and continental transport links, both the railroad and steamers, to more distant commercial hubs like Tacoma and Portland. Like other rural communities in the West, the Great Depression made life even more challenging. The onset of World War II, though, dramatically changed the lives of the residents of these towns. Initially, it meant the beginnings of recovery, as they were able to sell their crops for higher prices than in prior years. This recovery was brief, though, as the war led to the creation of the Hanford Site and the subsequent forced evacuation of the residents of these communities from their land. This volume will trace the history of these communities from their origins in the late nineteenth and early twentieth centuries, through their settlement and development, the arrival of irrigation, their dependence on the railroads, their struggles and survival during the Great Depression and, finally, to their unique experiences in the early years of World War II.

This monograph is based largely on extensive oral history interviews held at the Hanford History Project at Washington State University Tri-Cities. To date the Hanford History Project/Oral History Project has conducted over 170 interviews with pre-1943 residents and early Hanford workers. All of the oral histories and their transcripts are or will be available on the Hanford History Project website at HanfordHistory. org. In addition, archival research for this volume was conducted at the Hanford History Project Archive at WSU Tri-Cities, the Richland Public Library, the Department of Energy (DOE), Mission Support Alliance (MSA) records, and the East Benton County Historical Society and Museum (EBCHSM).

The editors and authors acknowledge an inherent bias in the oral histories upon which much of this volume and subsequent volumes are based. That bias is that virtually all of the oral histories conducted by the Hanford History Project—due to the age of the interviewees, geography, proximity, and cost—have been with former residents and Hanford workers who continue to live in eastern Washington. Many of the former residents of White Bluffs, Hanford, and Richland moved to the west side of the state or to other parts of the nation or world following their removal from their communities, or at some later date. For the most part, those who relocated far from central Washington have not been interviewed by this project, and it is possible that they may have had different perspectives on the communities and their significance than people who continued to live near those former town sites for the rest of their lives. In other words, they may have brought a certain perspective or distance, both geographical and emotional, that those living and working nearby could not or did not bring to their interviews.

In addition, certain caveats exist whenever scholars are relying on oral histories for their primary sources. The inherent biases of the interviewer, the fading memories of the interviewees, all of whom were at least in their early eighties at the time they were interviewed, the video recording of the interviews, and the location of the interviews in a studio. Each of these elements could, and likely did, influence the outcome of the oral histories, at least in small ways. The authors and editors have tried to take those issues into account by attempting to corroborate stories, and by using other primary sources, including letters, government reports, photographs, census records, and others—that may confirm or contradict those memories and stories. But, of course, because the towns no longer exist, and have not existed for over seventy years, oral histories of necessity remain the best way to chronicle the stories of these communities and the people who lived and worked there.

Importantly, this volume is not a part of a series on the Manhattan Project, although efforts at Hanford as part of the Manhattan Project certainly will be the focus of later volumes. In addition, this volume, while including discussions of the histories of Native peoples in the region, will not incorporate Native voices extensively. A future volume on race and diversity in the region will treat that subject in greater depth. Instead, this volume focuses on the unique story of Euro-American settlements in the Hanford region and the removal of those settlements and their inhabitants to make way for the nuclear reservation. In the process, it will emphasize the places of meaning that these residents lost and their attempts to remember those places.

It is important to note that racially these towns were almost exclusively white. While the West was the most racially diverse region in the United States in the late nineteenth and early twentieth centuries, the towns of Hanford, White Bluffs, and Richland did not reflect that diversity. Indeed, other than contacts and connections with local Wanapum families and individuals (some of whom are represented in this volume), residents of the towns of the Priest Rapids Valley rarely interacted with nonwhites. While the nearby town of Pasco included residents of Chinese and Japanese ancestry, those populations were relatively small, and Pasco was twenty to thirty miles away. Indeed, in the 1920s Priest Rapids Valley residents made concerted efforts to keep Japanese-American farmers out of the region, a development that will be addressed in the forthcoming volume on race and diversity in the region. In part as a result of those efforts, the towns of the Priest Rapids Valley remained almost entirely white.[10]

The first chapter in this volume covers the settlement of the three towns directly impacted by the Manhattan Project—White Bluffs, Hanford, and Richland. It addresses the methods of transportation and links to commercial centers that played a large role in the settlement of the West. It incorporates primary sources and important American West scholarship to examine the impact of wagon trade, steamships, and railroads in the region, grounding a local history in the larger context of American West history. In addition, this chapter examines the question: how does a public historian study and present the often forgotten past of the pre-1943 Hanford communities? Using his experiences with historic preservation, cultural resource management, and oral history at Hanford, David W. Harvey will discuss the challenges and opportunities of documenting and preserving the histories of the Wanapum community and the pre-1943 Euro-American communities of Hanford and White Bluffs. His chapter uses oral histories, cultural artifacts, and documents to explain how public historians have uncovered, studied, and presented both the Native and Euro-American communities that existed in the Hanford area before 1943.

Chapter two, written by Robert Franklin, details the struggles early residents faced while attempting to turn the eastern Washington scrubland into an agricultural Eden, and the tight bonds formed between residents of these remote and small towns. In the first four decades of the twentieth century farmers-to-be moved to the towns of Hanford, White Bluffs, and Richland to unlock the potential of irrigated land, in the process struggling against both the land and the capital companies that provided the irrigation. Using oral histories of early residents and primary source collections at the Hanford History Project, Franklin discusses the difficulty in irrigation farming and the development of commerce in these small towns, as well as institutions of social and community life such as churches, schools, and newspapers. As a public historian and assistant director of the Hanford History Project, Franklin provides a new perspective on the rural, agricultural West that links public and academic representations of the Hanford Site.

Chapter three, written by Laura Arata, considers the experiences of women who came to live and work in the communities of White Bluffs and Hanford between the turn of the twentieth century and the forced evacuation of the area in 1943. Before 1929, many women came to the area with parents or spouses and viewed their experiences as those of pioneers moving into a sparsely inhabited place for the purpose of settling it. During the 1930s others arrived as migrants in search of an escape from the desperate conditions created by the Great Depression, and found residents who welcomed them with open arms into a community surrounded by plentiful fruit orchards. Interviews and oral histories suggest that women experienced deep grief in response to mandatory removal in 1943 and internalized this profound sense of loss not in terms of wartime sacrifice, but as the painful and irreversible destruction of communities that could not be recreated in other locations. Considering the experiences of women in these communities adds important depth and nuance to the larger history of Hanford, which has often been viewed from the perspective of men's service. This chapter incorporates some of the significant scholarship on women in the American West to inform its discussion of gendered experiences in these rural areas. It addresses questions related to the gender role expectations for women in these towns and their importance to the agricultural economy and community life.

Chapter four, written by Robert Bauman, incorporates the voices of former residents of Richland, Hanford, and White Bluffs to tell the story of their forced removal from their land to make way for the Manhattan Project. It uses oral histories and other sources to demonstrate how residents were informed of their forced evacuation, how they responded to the news, and their efforts to receive adequate compensation for their land and properties. Displacement is a common theme in the American West. Native peoples, in particular, have experienced long histories of displacement at the hands of Euro-Americans and the federal government.

This chapter provides a unique example of that theme of displacement—both Native peoples and Euro-Americans being displaced at the hands of the federal government to make way for a secret wartime project—and examines the similarities and differences in the displacement of those groups. It uses oral histories, artifacts, and archival sources to explore the ways in which the removal of Native and Euro-American residents from Hanford, White Bluffs, and Richland both reflects and challenges traditional displacement stories in the American West and complicates our understanding of the Hanford Site.

Finally, the conclusion of this volume uses annual reunions of the former residents of the towns of Hanford and White Bluffs to explore issues of community and memory, and the ways in which the lives of the residents of the Priest Rapids Valley reflected the experiences of many Euro-American settlers in the American West. Additionally, it emphasizes the ways in which spaces and places of meaning—the buildings, the land, and the environment in which these people lived—were lost, and the ways in which the former residents of the towns in the Priest Rapids Valley attempted to remember those spaces and places.

Recent years have seen a "spatial turn" in historical scholarship, particularly scholarship on the American West. This historical literature emphasizes the importance of place and space in peoples' lives—the buildings, the land, the geography, and the environment of where they live. But how do we understand or learn about places and "spaces of meaning," like the towns of Hanford and White Bluffs that no longer exist? How do we, as one historian has asked, "make sense of places where the past has largely been erased or overlooked and its inhabitants disposed?" This volume attempts to do just that—uncover some of these spaces of meaning of towns, farms, and communities that no longer exist—through the memories and stories of the people who lived in these communities and whose families were removed from their land.[11]

Notes

1. Dick Wiehl, interview by Robert Bauman, Hanford History Project (HHP), June 5, 2013.

2. See Richard Rhodes, *The Making of the Atomic Bomb* (New York: Simon and Schuster, 1986); Michele Gerber, *On the Home Front: The Cold War Legacy of the Hanford Nuclear Site* (Lincoln: University of Nebraska Press, 1992); Michael D'Antonio, *Atomic Harvest: Hanford and the Lethal Toll of America's Nuclear Arsenal* (New York: Crown, 1993); and Kate Brown, *Plutopia: Nuclear Families, Atomic Cities, and the Great Soviet and American Plutonium Disasters* (New York: Oxford University Press, 2013).

3. Patricia Nelson Limerick, "The Significance of Hanford in American History," in Paul Hirt, ed., *Terra Pacifica: People and Place in the Northwest States and Canada* (Pullman: WSU Press, 1998), 53–70. Quotes are from pages 59 and 61.

4. Brian Freer, "Atomic Pioneers and Environmental Legacy at the Hanford Site," *Canadian Review of Sociology and Anthropology* 31, no. 3 (August 1994), 305–24; Robert Bauman, "Jim Crow in the Tri-Cities, 1943–1950," *Pacific Northwest Quarterly* 96, no. 3 (Summer 2005), 124–31; John M. Findlay and Bruce Hevly, *Atomic Frontier Days: Hanford and the American West* (Seattle: Center for the Study of the Pacific Northwest and University of Washington Press, 2011); and Lee Ann Powell, "Culture, Cold War, Conservatism, and the End of the Atomic Age: Richland, Washington, 1943–1989" (PhD diss., Washington State University, 2013).

5. See Frederick Jackson Turner, "The Significance of the Frontier in American History," Annual Report of the American Historical Association, 1893. Reprint by University Microfilms, 1966.

6. Walter Prescott Webb, *The Great Plains* (Boston: Ginn and Company, 1931).

7. Donald W. Meinig, *The Great Columbia Plain: A Historical Geography, 1805–1910* (Seattle: University of Washington Press, 1968).

8. Mark Fiege, *Irrigated Eden: The Making of an Agricultural Landscape in the American West* (Seattle: University of Washington Press, 1999).

9. Donald Worster, *Rivers of Empire: Water, Aridity and the Growth of the American West* (New York: Pantheon Books, 1985); Leah S. Glaser, *Electrifying the Rural American West: Stories of Power, People and Place* (Lincoln: University of Nebraska Press, 2009); Lawrence J. MacDonnell, *From Reclamation to Sustainability: Water, Agriculture and the Environment in the American West* (Niwot: University Press of Colorado, 1999).

10. A seminal study on the unique, multiracial history of the American West is Richard White, "Race Relations in the American West," *American Quarterly* 38, no. 3 (1986): 396–416.

11. The term "spaces of meaning" is from Robert Self, *American Babylon: Race and the Struggle for Postwar Oakland* (Princeton University Press, 2003). The quote "make sense of places..." is from Steven Hoelscher's review of Kate Brown, *Dispatches from Dystopia: Histories of Places Not Yet Forgotten* (University of Chicago Press, 2014) in *The Public Historian* 39, no. 1 (February 2017), 103. See Brown's book, particularly chapter one, for more on these overlooked spaces and their significance.

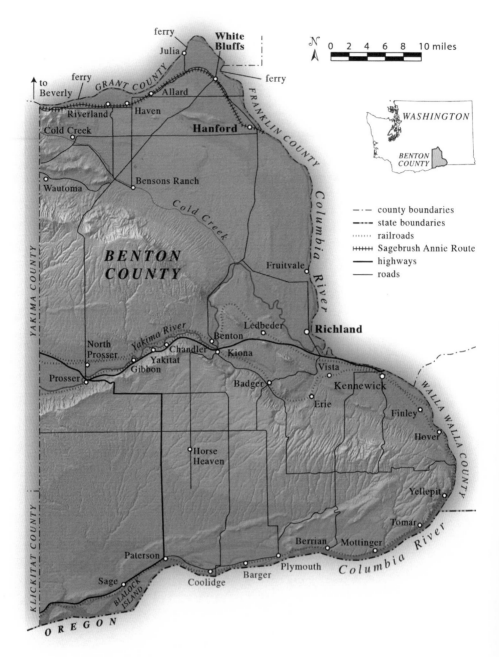

Benton County, Washington, showing the "Sagebrush Annie" railroad spur of the transcontinental Chicago, Milwaukee, St. Paul and Pacific Railroad, which travelled south along the Columbia River from Beverly, through Riverland, Haven, Allard, and White Bluffs to Hanford. *Map by Chelsea Feeney, cmcfeeney.com based on Washington Department of Highways, Map of Benton County, 1932, rev. 1937. MASC, Washington State University Libraries.*

CHAPTER ONE

An Oasis in the Desert?

White Bluffs, Hanford, and Richland, The Early Years

David W. Harvey

The United States government established the Hanford Engineer Works in 1943 in Richland, Washington, as a top-secret Manhattan Project site for the production of plutonium for the nation's first atomic bombs during the Second World War. Plutonium production continued throughout the Cold War era until the 1980s at what later became known as the U.S. Department of Energy's (DOE's) Hanford Site. At the same time, Hanford became one of the richest cultural resources areas in the Columbia Plateau. The existence of considerably intact cultural resources is due to the fact that Hanford has essentially been off limits to the public since 1943, with no agricultural, recreational, or residential development at the site. Only a small percentage of Hanford's 560 square miles was developed for plutonium production and disposal of radioactive and non-radioactive wastes.

While the Hanford Site no longer produces nuclear materials, it has been the focus of intensive environmental cleanup since the late 1980s. The environmental cleanup of the Hanford Site resulted in the need for the DOE to document, interpret, and preserve important prehistoric and historic period archaeological remains and built environments that could be adversely impacted during cleanup efforts. Since its establishment in 1966, the National Historic Preservation Act (NHPA) has required all federal agencies like the DOE to determine if cultural resources under their control are eligible for listing in the National Register of Historic

Places (NRHP). Thus, in 1989 DOE established the Hanford Site Cultural and Historical Resources Program in the Pacific Northwest National Laboratory (PNNL) to document and assess cultural resources at Hanford. Battelle Memorial Institute has managed PNNL since it was established by the Atomic Energy Commission in 1965.

The Hanford Site comprises a series of cultural landscapes containing the cumulative record of multiple occupations by both Native Americans and Euro-Americans. For management and interpretive purposes, these cultural landscapes are divided into the Native American, the Early Settlers/Farming, and the Manhattan Project and Cold War eras. Well-preserved archaeological and above-ground cultural resources include the remains and landscapes of pre-1943 farms, town sites, orchards, crops, canals, residential and agricultural foundations, irrigation facilities, Manhattan Project and Cold War era buildings and artifacts, and precontact and Wanapum Indian cultural remains.

The well-preserved surface remains and archaeological resources illustrate the lifestyles and occupations of the pre-1943 farms and town sites at the Hanford Site, where the desert was transformed through irrigation into productive farmland. During the late 1930s and early 1940s the Priest Rapids Valley was coming out of the Great Depression. By 1943, many of the farms and orchards were producing fruit, agricultural fields had rows of crops and vegetables, lawns and gardens surrounded homes, and new businesses were opening in White Bluffs and Hanford. Upon condemnation by the government many of the pre-1943 extant cultural resources became frozen in time, including refuse dumps, fence lines, crop rows, farm machinery, building foundations, orchards, and root cellars. Hanford is one of the few places in North America where the intact remains of over one hundred farms from the first several decades of the twentieth century exist.

The focus of this chapter is the documentation and interpretation of the Early Settlers/Farming landscape at Hanford Site, including the establishment and evolution of the three communities—Hanford, White Bluffs, and Richland—directly impacted by the Manhattan Project. These three communities were comprised of those areas on the Hanford Site where people, mainly of European descent, settled in the Columbia River Plateau prior to the start of the Manhattan Project during 1943.

Non-Native American presence in the mid-Columbia began with the arrival of the Lewis and Clark Expedition in 1805. But it was not until the late nineteenth and early twentieth centuries that non-Native American peoples began intensive settlement on the Hanford Site. A record of their activities and land use is present in the archaeological sites, traditional cultural places, and buildings and structures that are located throughout the Hanford Site, specifically in the vicinity of the former communities of Hanford and White Bluffs. The remains of approximately one hundred Hanford and White Bluffs farms and irrigation facilities and several non-Indian town sites have been the focus of continuous documentation and mitigation by Battelle and PNNL cultural resource management staff. As part of this effort, a historic context for the Euro-American settlement period (pre-Hanford era) has been prepared as part of a National Register Multiple Property Documentation form to assist with the evaluation of the National Register eligibility of historic archaeological resources, traditional cultural places, and historic period structures.

Public history and cultural resources management efforts have led to the establishment of Manhattan Project National Historic Park at Hanford, a discontiguous national park that also includes Manhattan Project sites at Los Alamos, New Mexico, and Oak Ridge, Tennessee. At Hanford, the park includes the interpretation and management of the cultural landscapes and remains of the Hanford and White Bluffs town sites and Wanapum Indian communities. Besides interpreting the significance of the Manhattan Project at Hanford, the National Park Service (NPS) will interpret the lifestyles and histories of the pre-1943 communities and their sacrifices (i.e. their homes and properties condemned for the war effort). Interpretation of the histories and lifestyles of the inhabitants of the three pre-1943 Hanford Site communities directly impacted by the Manhattan Project has been aided significantly by the recording of the oral histories of the community's inhabitants and their descendants, originally by PNNL and other community groups, and currently conducted by the Washington State University (WSU) Hanford History Project.

When Euro-Americans started arriving in what was to become known as the Priest Rapids Valley, they found a landscape basically unchanged for thousands of years. Pleistocene floods of massive extent shaped much of the Mid-Columbia Plateau, the last of which occurred approximately

12,000 years ago.[1] Distinctive characteristics of the resultant arid land-scape are a considerable lack of moisture, extreme heat and cold, sandy soil, and large rivers fed by mountain streams and snow melt. Commonly referred to as a shrub steppe environment, it was originally dominated by sagebrush and bunchgrasses.[2] The lifeways of both the indigenous people and the Euro-American explorers and settlers were significantly shaped by this desert landscape. It was the Euro-Americans who considerably modified the desert to accommodate their transportation, agricultural, and town building activities.

Prior to the arrival of Euro-Americans, Indians had lived along the Columbia River for at least the past 10,000 years. These earliest residents were the ancestors to the present-day Wanapum, whose villages and fishing camps were found along the Columbia River from Priest Rapids to present-day Richland.[3] When non-Indian settlement of the Mid-Columbia began, the Wanapum were living mainly at Priest Rapids, and utilized seasonal fishing and gathering camps at White Bluffs, Horn Rapids (on the Yakima River), and as far south as Columbia Point

Wanapum tule reed houses on beach, near Priest Rapids, Columbia River, Washington, circa 1941. *University of Washington Libraries, Special Collections, no. 564: Db-31.*

in Richland.[4] Neighboring Indian groups such as the Yakama, Umatilla, Cayuse, Walla Walla, Palus, Nez Perce, and Salish frequented the area to trade and conduct seasonal hunting and gathering activities.[5]

The men of the Lewis and Clark expedition (1804–1806) were some of the first Euro-Americans to explore the Mid-Columbia Plateau.[6] In 1811 explorer David Thompson of the North West Company became the first non-Indian to travel the entire length of the Columbia River, passing through the future town sites of White Bluffs, Hanford, and Richland

Horse-powered ferry at White Bluffs, circa 1909. *Hanford History Project, Harry and Juanita Anderson Collection, RG41_1084.*

on his way to the mouth of the Columbia River.[7] The fur companies and other explorers soon followed as they sought trade goods from the region's tribes. The fur companies established trading posts and routes across the interior, which attracted trappers, military units, and miners to the Mid-Columbia.

By the mid-nineteenth century the discovery of gold on the upper Columbia River and in British Columbia brought thousands of miners into the region. Merchants and cattle and sheep ranchers soon followed to supply the miners with goods and services. Steamboat transportation developed on the Columbia River, and communities sprang up to serve the miners heading north.[8] The high retail prices in the mining camps and lowered transportation costs due to the steamboats attracted farmers and livestock producers to the region.[9] Steamboat transportation increased the construction of connecting roads for the transport of settlers and supplies to the interior, eventually leading to the founding of interior

Ferry "Doris," Hanford, WA, no date. *Hanford History Project, Harry and Juanita Anderson Collection, RG41_035.*

Steamboat on the Columbia River near White Bluffs, no date. *Hanford History Project, Harry and Juanita Anderson Collection, RG41_1074.*

frontier settlements like White Bluffs, as described in PNNL's application for listing in the National Register of Historic Places:

> A ferry started operating at White Bluffs in 1858 to assist those heading to the mines. White Bluffs quickly became an important point for the transfer of goods (headed to the interior gold fields), and one of the first permanent non-Indian settlements in the Priest Rapids Valley. Pack trains heading north to supply the mining camps used the ferry, and by the late 1850s White Bluffs became the furthest upriver stopping point for steamboats.[10]

Beldin's Store, Hanford, 1935. *Hanford History Project, Harry and Juanita Anderson Collection, RG41_1336.*

Overall growth of early non-Indian settlements in the Priest Rapids Valley was tied to improvements in transportation systems that would provide an outlet for profitable cash exports. Primary reliance on wagon routes and pack trails often obstructed the development of communities and diverse export economies beyond the mere frontier subsistence level.[11] Due to the transitory nature of frontier communities, road systems sometimes became obsolete before their completion. The arrival of the

Downtown White Bluffs, 1918. *Hanford History Project, Harry and Juanita Anderson Collection, RG41_1258.*

steamboat on the Mid-Columbia brought greater economic stability to the region by providing more reliable service for developing local businesses and communities, and a faster vehicle for the export of commodities and goods.[12]

Despite the establishment of communities in the Priest Rapids Valley during the last quarter of the nineteenth century, extensive settlement of lands between Hanford and Richland lagged behind adjacent valleys, primarily due to the Priest Rapids Valley's harsh, arid environment and the lack of easily obtained irrigation water. "Farmers migrating west by-passed Hanford and White Bluffs for homesteads that had better access to water and dry-land farming opportunities in areas such as the upland sections of the Walla Walla and Yakima River valleys," noted the PNNL report.[13]

The beginning of the last quarter of the nineteenth century saw considerable growth of livestock ranching, with a subsequent increase in community development on the Mid-Columbia. The region's abundant grasslands provided excellent terrain for the grazing of cattle, sheep, and horses. While the open range lasted into the early twentieth century, the devastating winters of the 1880s decimated livestock herds to such an extent that they never fully recovered.[14] Some ranchers turned to cultivating small family farms. The majority of the new settlers were interested in farming, and their arrival hastened the transition of the regional economy from stock raising to agriculture. The early twentieth century featured a widespread growth of agriculture, with an increasing dependency on irrigation.[15] The arrival of irrigation led to rapid population increases in the Priest Rapids Valley. By 1910, Hanford had a population of approximately 370, while White Bluffs had approximately 325.

The most pressing need of settlers coming to the region was to develop irrigation systems. At first, they irrigated individually or formed cooperatives, but many of these initial enterprises failed because they were undercapitalized. The coming of the railroads and federal legislation enabled the establishment and funding of larger irrigation projects that created an attractive environment for the cultivation and export of agricultural produce. The transcontinental railroads brought settlers and sold them railroad-owned lands. The railroads also provided the means to export the farmer's produce to urban markets across the country. The increasing number of homesteaders, as well as the use of barbed wire and fencing of cultivated fields, brought to an end the dominance of ranching. Family farms and towns grew rapidly.

The introduction of irrigated agriculture during the late 1880s and early 1890s changed agricultural practices and settlement patterns in the Priest Rapids Valley. Irrigation allowed for the expansion of farms and cultivation of more crops and produce, both for local consumption and shipment to distant markets via the railroads. Local population increased in rural and urban centers as irrigation attracted more settlers and farmers. Town populations increased to provide services for the farming populations. Pasco, Kennewick, and Ainsworth were founded in the mid-1880s after the arrival of the Northern Pacific Railroad in 1882. The region attracted farmers because its fruit growing season was longer than other areas in eastern Washington. Early fruit growers were aware that the Priest Rapids Valley produced crops two to three weeks earlier than other fruit-growing areas.[16] Large-scale agriculture, however, was not achieved in the Priest Rapids Valley until enactment of the Newlands Reclamation Act in 1902, which provided federal financing of local irrigation projects.[17] The act was heralded by President Theodore Roosevelt as "a policy more important to the country's internal development than any since the

Homestead Law of Lincoln's time."[18] According to former resident Donald Evett, expansion of irrigation due to the federal legislation allowed his parents to plant a successful fruit orchard in the Priest Rapids Valley.[19]

The anticipation and subsequent completion of large-scale irrigation projects by early settlers led to the founding and growth of Richland. Early residents like Ben Rosencrance attempted to use the Yakima River to irrigate their homesteads to grow hay, grain, vegetables, and fruit trees.

> Rosencrance had been ranching on the south side of the Yakima River since 1880, but in 1888 he moved across the river to the present site of Richland. He filed a homestead claim of 1,700 acres and soon other farmers followed, including Nelson Rich who also established a homestead nearby.[20]

The Rich and Rosencrance farmsteads at the confluence of the Yakima and Columbia Rivers were the setting of some of the first attempts at irrigation in the lower Yakima River Valley. Rosencrance and Rich along with other early settlers constructed water wheels along the banks of the Yakima that lifted the water out of the river into a system of flumes and ditches or canals.[21]

In 1904 W. R. Amon and his son Howard moved to the area and purchased the Rosencrance and Rich homesteads. The Amons founded the town site of Richland in 1905 (incorporated in 1910) and formed the Benton Water Company to provide electricity and irrigation to the town.[22] A few years later, the Benton Water Company merged with the Lower Yakima Irrigation Company, which led to the construction of the Richland Irrigation Canal. The canal, fifteen miles long, was the first in the region to deliver irrigation water over a large area, specifically lands west of the Columbia River in North Richland.[23] Historian Barb Kubik wrote:

> Richland grew into a small and prosperous agricultural community in the early years of World War I. Despite the fact that the town was unable to attract a railroad, a small business district thrived along the town's main street…agricultural prices and the value of farm land rose steadily during the war years, and Richland continued to produce early, quality fruit, vegetables and poultry.[24]

Lacking railroad access because trains were routed through Pasco and Kennewick, Richland remained smaller than Hanford or White Bluffs. All three communities were platted during the first decade of the twentieth century, but were established and experienced considerable growth during the last decade of the nineteenth century.[25] Bridges over the Yakima frequently washed out until a more permanent one was constructed over the Yakima River delta that connected Richland and Kennewick in 1907.[26] The Timmerman family, early settlers on the lower Yakima River, established a cable ferry at Columbia Point in 1894 connecting Richland and Pasco. The ferry continued in use into the early 1930s when it terminated operations due to the construction of an automobile bridge over the Columbia River. By 1920 the population of Richland was 279, but it saw dramatic growth during the next several years until the Great Depression.[27]

As in Richland, the anticipation of large-scale irrigation projects in the upper Priest Rapids Valley led to an increase in new settlers establishing farmsteads near Hanford and White Bluffs. Sensing an opportunity, the Hanford Irrigation and Power Company (HIPC) organized in Seattle for the purpose of reclaiming 32,000 acres of arid land near White Bluffs and Hanford, including the planned construction of a pumping plant upriver at Coyote Rapids and a major irrigation canal to deliver water to Hanford and White Bluffs farms. This created a frenzy of construction of residences and farms and orchard development in the valley.

Murrel Dawson, former Priest Rapids Valley resident, spent her very early years at Hanford prior to her family's move upriver to Priest Rapids in 1941 where her father took a job as an operator at the Priest Rapids Power Plant. Dawson recalled:

> I went and finished my kindergarten there at Hanford. My dad hired on then at Priest Rapids as an operator at the little powerhouse. And they needed an operator…and Dad needed a job…he had some experience at that. But during the Depression days, like everyone else, he just hustled for work, because we had four children in the family at that time.[28]

Dawson remembered how the power plant generated electricity for the Coyote Rapids/Allard Pumping Plant located sixteen miles downstream from Priest Rapids. Electricity enabled the plant to pump water into the Hanford Irrigation Canal, providing water to the farms downstream in Hanford and White Bluffs. The construction of the Coyote Rapids Pumping Plant in 1908–9 marked the first large-scale effort to irrigate and provide a constant volume of water to farms between White Bluffs and Hanford.

Interestingly, Dawson was employed years later as an archaeological assistant for the Cultural Resources Program at PNNL that recorded the Coyote Rapids Pumping Plant and the Hanford Irrigation Canal. Besides documenting their significance for providing irrigation water to downstream farms between White Bluffs and Hanford that led to considerable growth of the communities, the cultural resources program's documentation led to a determination of NRHP eligibility of the pumping plant and canal for the role they played in the growth and development of the farms and communities on the Mid-Columbia. Documenting the history and significance of the pumping plant and canal assisted in their preservation as important components of the pre-1943 non-Indian settlement of the Priest Rapids Valley. The pumping plant and canal continue to play a key role in telling the story of the pre-1943 growth of irrigation and settlement of Hanford and White Bluffs for the NPS's Manhattan Project National Historic Park.

Anticipation of the canal delivering substantial amounts of irrigated water led to the incorporation of Richland, White Bluffs, and Hanford as new settlers arrived in large numbers to establish farms and orchards. Most lived in those three communities. More than 1,000 people lived in the Priest Rapids Valley by 1910.[29] Initially the canal was not a success, as there were numerous breaches and unlined portions of the canal allowed for the loss of excessive water due to its seepage into the soil. The consequent lack of irrigated water led to the failure of many orchards. A number of farmers sued the irrigation company for their losses. Ultimately the irrigation company lined the entire canal with concrete and the breaches (and lawsuits) were eliminated.

The growth of agriculture and settlement was aided significantly by the arrival of transcontinental railroad and branch lines in the Mid-Columbia basin. Although steamboat transportation revolutionized the transporting of people and freight, the railroads could export products and produce more efficiently and at less expense. They could also transport people in greater numbers.[30] The growth of the Hanford and White Bluffs area was stimulated by the construction of a branch line of the transcontinental Chicago, Milwaukee, St. Paul and Pacific Railroad from

Coyote Rapids Pumping Plant, also known as the Allard Pump House, constructed 1908. *National Park Service.*

Beverly, Washington, to White Bluffs and Hanford. Known affectionately as "Sagebrush Annie," the Priest Rapids Valley branch train "enabled the farmers to ship large quantities of fruit and other produce to distant markets via a transcontinental railroad."[31] Murrel Dawson remembered that "Sagebrush Annie just came down and picked up the fruit at Vernita and White Bluffs and turned around and went back."[32]

Community leaders and real estate interests eagerly tried to persuade railroads to locate their lines and stations near their communities. News of the railroad passing close to White Bluffs prompted the residents to move the town from the west bank of the Columbia River approximately one mile inland to the location of the soon-to-be-built railroad station. Relocation of communities to take advantage of an anticipated rail line was common throughout the American West into the early twentieth century. The motives were usually economic—to increase commerce and trade and sell land. Real estate interests and railroads sought to capitalize on their investments adjacent to an anticipated rail line, and sell railroad-owned lands to newly-arrived settlers. East White Bluffs, the original settlement across the Columbia at the foot of the bluffs, had in

1907 moved across the river to the west bank, where it was less prone to flooding. The move also allowed the two to grow. The narrow strip of land on the east bank between the river and the bluffs had become overcrowded as land promotions and irrigation development attracted an unsustainable number of new settlers.

The availability of irrigated water made the Priest Rapids Valley one of the premier orchard regions in eastern Washington by the second decade of the twentieth century. Walt Grisham remarked how his family had "seven acres of peaches, four acres of apricots, and two acres of grapes. Most of the farms were pretty well diversified, we had a pasture, hay... we had as much as four–five cows."[33] Former Hanford resident Rod Bunnell remembered how the land around Hanford and White Bluffs was "wide open," with a plethora of lots for locating homes and farmsteads: "Hanford was obviously laid out by an optimistic developer and not all the lots were sold."[34] Farmsteads and homes were spread out among the unsold properties at Hanford and throughout the Mid-Columbia. This was not surprising, considering community boosterism and land promo-

Sagebrush Annie, Hanford and White Bluffs, circa 1920s. *Hanford History Project, Harry and Juanita Anderson Collection, RG41_1154.*

tions by developers, real estate interests, and railroads began in the region as early as the 1890s.

During the first couple of decades of the twentieth century, there was ceaseless advertising to attract settlers to a "promised land" of irrigated farmlands and growing communities in the arid West. Likewise, the Priest Rapids Valley offered promises of a desert oasis. Promotion of the Mid-Columbia was lavish, and land companies, railroads, and real estate interests prepared brochures touting the region's bountiful fruit and vegetable harvests.[35] This boosterism helped fuel the region's irrigation and settlement boom, as the area experienced its largest popula-

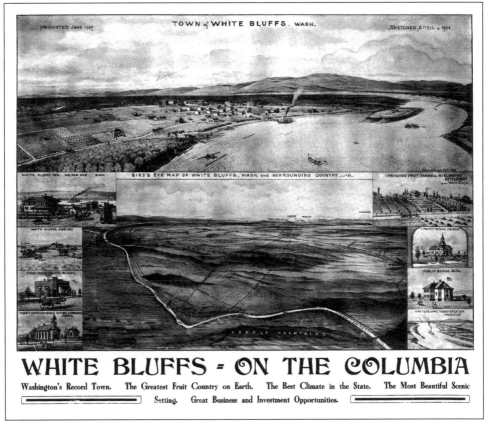

Promotion of White Bluffs, circa 1915. *East Benton County Historical Society and Museum.*

tion expansion. Land promotions to attract settlers to the Priest Rapids Valley began soon after the arrival of transcontinental railroads to the Mid-Columbia (with the first transcontinental railroad arriving in Pasco in 1882). In his interview in 2013, former resident Dick Wiehl recalled how his grandfather arrived in the Priest Rapids Valley during the late nineteenth century and settled at East White Bluffs: "My grandfather… came in the late 1890s, and it was the result of advertisement, which was nationwide. And he came out with the prospect of buying some acreage… and he established a ranch."[36]

The transcontinental railroads conducted a nationwide campaign to attract new settlers to the Priest Rapids Valley. The railroads had a vested interest in transporting new settlers to the Mid-Columbia in an attempt to recoup the costs of constructing their rail lines. The Northern Pacific Railroad had a real estate division that had acquired tracts of land in the Priest Rapids Valley, and aggressively advertised "cheap land" and touted/boostered the benefits of the farm land and communities on the Mid-Columbia to potential settlers nationwide.

Community boosterism continued during World War I as Europe's increased need for foodstuffs during the war contributed to a considerable demand for American agricultural products. Many American farmers, including those along the Mid-Columbia, prospered due to the high prices they received for their goods during the war. "By 1920, there were approximately 150 irrigated farms in the Hanford and White Bluffs area."[37] Former resident Edith King remembers her parents acquiring property at Hanford from several businessmen in Seattle who were promoting Priest Rapids Valley lands: "They pawned that off on my dad but it was a good place to live."[38] Former resident Robert Fletcher, who was born in 1922 shortly after his parents arrived in Richland from Walla Walla, remembers his parents were attracted to Kennewick and Richland:

> Because irrigation water was being made available from the rivers… There were private developers and they would get bonds backed by the state government…there were brochures that these companies would advertise…come to Kennewick and Richland, that was available, the climate was ideal, and the soil was great, and you could make a living on just a few acres if you know how to farm. So, my dad bought 20 acres of sagebrush.[39]

Former resident Morris Slavens recalls that his parents decided to move to Hanford (from nearby Pasco) in 1912, based on promotions advertising the expansion of irrigated lands in the Priest Rapids Valley. They traveled on a sternwheeler upriver to the Hanford ferry landing, and acquired "9 acres where they raised apples and alfalfa and miscellaneous fruits."[40]

Local real estate companies, railroads, and the chambers of commerce hired famed photographer Asahel Curtis to capture through his photographs the "bountiful agricultural cornucopia" of the Priest Rapids Valley, and the benefits of locating businesses and farms in the Mid-Columbia.[41] Besides White Bluffs and Hanford, Richland was also the focus of the promotional frenzy to attract new settlers to the region. Settlement of Richland was enhanced as a result of the Northern Pacific's promotion of its transcontinental railroad to Kennewick and Pasco during the late nineteenth century. The local business community advertised that "Richland is certain to be one of the most important towns on the Columbia River surrounded as it is by 16,000 acres of the finest irrigated lands in the West."[42]

The high prices for agricultural produce that farmers received during World War I did not last. Postwar agricultural prosperity suffered when demand for agricultural products lessened during the 1920s. The economic depression that most of the country suffered during the 1930s hit the nation's farmers earlier, including those in the Priest Rapids Valley.

By the 1920s the era of limitless land and railroad expansion was over in eastern Washington and throughout the arid West.[43] The "wet years" of increased precipitation that dominated the arid West during the first two decades of the twentieth century had encouraged homesteading on marginal lands. Those years, however, were followed by a decade of typical dry climatic conditions and a reduction of irrigated lands, which partly led to the rural depression of the 1920s, numerous foreclosures, and the Great Depression of the 1930s.[44]

The depressed postwar economic conditions in the Priest Rapids Valley did not deter real estate promoters and land colonization efforts. One example was the soldier settlements program, a combination of postwar assistance to World War I veterans and continual efforts to expand irrigation of arid lands. The State of Washington enacted the Land Settlement Act in 1919, or the White Bluffs-Hanford Land Settlement Project, which offered more than 2,000 acres in twenty-acre plots at very low cost to wartime veterans who aspired to be farmers.[45] The soldier settlement tracts came with a house, barn, chicken house, and a well for both drinking and irrigation use. Veterans were also offered loans for fencing, land-clearing, seed, and electricity.[46] The first sixty-nine veterans moved onto their lots in 1922.

Former Hanford-White Bluffs resident Yvonne McGee remembered her father, a World War I veteran, qualified for one of the tracts on a low-cost loan basis, and the twenty-acre plots were located in the White Bluffs-Hanford Valley. Unfortunately, most of the veterans had limited experience as farmers.[47] According to PNNL:

> By 1924, thirty-nine of the soldier settlements still remained unsold, which the state disposed of at a public auction. Persistent drought, falling crop prices, and difficulties in cultivating the Hanford-White Bluffs soil led to numerous defaults by the time of the Great Depression. By 1934, only sixteen of the original sixty-nine soldier settlers remained on the tracts.[48]

The Great Depression of the 1930s reduced the price of crops and land values, severely affecting the economic fortunes of the Mid-Columbia. Nevertheless, depressed economic conditions still "did not deter real estate promoters and land colonization efforts. Representatives of the Northern Pacific Railroad and other independent colonizers continued to tout the grand qualities of the region in attempts to recruit new farmers to the area."[49] Even with the influx of some new settlers the area's economy continued to decline during the 1930s. The population decreased, numerous farms in the Mid-Columbia foreclosed, and many stores were vacant in White Bluffs, Hanford, and Richland. Farmers were receiving such low prices for their crops that much of the agricultural land was not under cultivation. Most residents who owned farms had to supplement their incomes with non-agricultural employment, and even bartering to make ends meet.

Former residents recollected that while the Depression was an extremely tough time, living on farms in the Priest Rapids Valley at least allowed inhabitants the opportunity to grow much of their own food. Former Hanford-White Bluffs resident Walt Grisham recalled that "this was a tremendously tough depression. The 30s were very tough, tough times…the best place you could have been at that time during the Depression was on the farm. At least you could grow some of your own food."[50]

Morris Slavens expressed similar sentiments: "There really wasn't very much employment for individuals…not much point going somewhere else because the Depression at that time was nationwide…at least you could raise a garden for fruit and vegetables and things weren't too expensive."[51]

Robert Fletcher recalled how there was limited access to electricity "until Roosevelt got the REA [Rural Electrification Act] started…and you got an electric pump to pump water up into a tank. And then you had pressure to run the water from the tank into the house…and so we had running water, we had an indoor bathroom…we got an electric stove… quite an improvement over the wood stove.[52]

During the Depression many Priest Rapids Valley residents abandoned their farms as they were unable to keep up payments on their mortgages and taxes. Rod Bunnell's father worked for the local power company, Pacific, Power & Light, and often the company had a lien for unpaid electric bills. Bunnell's father would then "go to the tax sale and bid on the lien and the power company would take title to the property."[53] He would then "try to find somebody to come in and take it over and farm it again."[54]

Some of the former residents expressed that while the local farms provided most of the food needs for the community during the Depression, a lot of people were still on relief or welfare. However, there were opportunities for employment working on government projects such as rebuilding schools and community centers, and work on county road projects. Assistance from New Deal programs helped Richland construct a community pool, a local bond issue funded the construction of a grade school, and city roads were graded and improved.[55] Local irrigation districts still attempted to bring more water to farmers, and some businesses did survive the Depression.

When World War II began, economic conditions started to improve in the Priest Rapids Valley. Wartime industries in eastern Washington and construction of the Grand Coulee Dam and the Columbia Basin irrigation projects enhanced the local and statewide economy and provided a sense of optimism in the Mid-Columbia communities.

The construction of the Grand Coulee Dam provided numerous jobs for previously unemployed residents throughout eastern Washington, including those living in the Priest Rapids Valley.[56] The dam generated an enormous amount of electrical power and made the Columbia Basin Irrigation Project possible.[57] Many local residents viewed these federal public works programs as having the greatest impact in helping the region out of the Depression. They looked favorably upon future dam construction and development of port facilities and reservoirs as means to directly stimulate the local economies by permitting upriver shipping by large vessels that would greatly assist the exporting of agricultural produce from the Priest Rapids Valley.[58]

The nationwide assistance of the war effort in Europe during the early 1940s directly benefited the Priest Rapids Valley, including area farmers. "Harvests in the Hanford district were bountiful in 1940, 1941 and 1942," reported PNNL, "and the Farm Security Administration offered loans to help growers expand production. After the war began, skilled agricultural workers were urged not to leave their farms as orchard owners scrambled to find workers."[59]

In 1942, the area saw its first military use when the U.S. Navy selected Pasco as the locale for an aviation training base for inexperienced pilots.[60] At the same time the War Department established the U.S. Army's Yakima Firing Center located just northwest of the future Hanford site in the ridges separating the Yakima and Ellensburg Valleys.[61]

During the early 1940s, even as the region experienced the anxieties and economic concerns with wartime food and gas rationing, there was a general optimism in the Priest Rapids Valley that better times lay ahead. Agricultural exports were increasing and unemployment was decreasing. This all came to a dramatic halt when local residents received official condemnation notices from the U.S. government in March 1943. Farmers and merchants, families and friends—all would have to abandon their homes, businesses, and properties for the war effort.

Notes

1. John Eliot Allen, Marjorie Burns, and Sam C. Sargent, *Cataclysms on the Columbia* (Portland: Timber Press, Inc., 1986), offers a fine summation of this unique series of floods based on the extensive scientific literature.

2. Rexford F. Daubenmire, *Steppe Vegetation of Washington*, Technical Bulletin 62 (Experimental Station, Washington State University, Pullman, 1970), 4.

3. Pacific Northwest National Laboratory, *The Hanford and White Bluffs Agricultural Landscape: Evaluation for Listing in the National Register of Historic Places*, for U. S. Department of Energy, Hanford Cultural and Historic Resources Program (Richland, WA, 2003), 11. Hereafter, PNNL, *Hanford and White Bluffs*.

4. Ibid.

5. Duane Alan Neitzel, *Hanford Site NEPA Characterization Report*, Rev. 17, PNNL-6415 (Richland, WA: Pacific Northwest National Laboratory, 2005), 16.

6. Gary Moulton, ed., *The Journals of the Lewis and Clark Expedition*, 13 vols. (Lincoln: University of Nebraska Press, 1983–2001), 5:162.

7. Jack Nisbet and Jack McMaster, *Sources of the River: Tracking David Thompson Across Western North America* (Seattle: Sasquatch Books, 1994), 28.

8. David W. Harvey, *Resource Protection Planning Process (RP3) Study Unit—Transportation* (Washington State Department of Community Development, Office of Archaeology and Historic Preservation, 1989), 7.

9. Philip R. P. Coelho and Katherine H. Daigle, "The Effects of Development in Transportation on the Settlement of the Inland Empire," *Agricultural History*, 56, no. 1 (January 1982): 22–36.

10. PNNL, *Hanford and White Bluffs*, 13.

11. Harvey, *Resource Protection Planning Process*, 7.

12. Ibid.

13. PNNL, *Hanford and White Bluffs*, 13–14.

14. Ibid.

15. James C. Chatters, ed., "History of Cultural Resources Management Activity on the Hanford Site," *Hanford Cultural Resources Management Plan*, PNL-6942 (Richland, WA: Pacific Northwest Laboratory, 1989), D.71.

16. James Sharpe, *Pre-Hanford Agricultural History—1900-1943*, BHI-01326 (Richland, WA: Bechtel Hanford Inc., 1999), 76.

17. Chatters, ed., "History of Cultural Resources Management Activity," D.67.

18. Click Relander, *Drummers and Dreamers* (Seattle: Northwest National Park and Forest Association, 1986), 147.

19. Donald Evett, interview by Ellen Prendergast, Hanford Cultural Resources Laboratory Oral History Program (HCRL), 2003. See chapter 2 for more on irrigation in the Priest Rapids Valley.

20. Jim Kershner, "Richland—Thumbnail History," *HistoryLink.org Essay* (File 8450, 2008), 2.

21. Barbara Kubik, *Richland—Celebrating Its Heritage* (City of Richland, WA, 1994), 9.

22. Kershner, "Richland," 2008, 3.

23. C. Landreau, *Historic Property Inventory Report—Richland Ditch* (Olympia, WA: Office of Archaeology and Historic Preservation, 2009), 4.

24. Kubik, *Richland*, 24.

25. Kershner, "Richland," 3.

26. Ibid.

27. Kubik, *Richland*, 25.

28. Murrel Dawson, interview by Robert Bauman, Hanford History Project (HHP), August 6, 2013.

29. PNNL, *Hanford and White Bluffs*, 16.

30. Meinig, *The Great Columbia Plain* (Seattle: University of Washington Press, 1968), 68.

31. PNNL, *Hanford and White Bluffs*, 17.

32. Murrel Dawson interview.

33. Walt Grisham, interview by Robert Bauman, HCRL, September 20, 2000.

34. Rod Bunnel, interview by Ellen Prendergast, HCRL, June 19, 2001.

35. Ibid.

36. Dick Wiehl, interview by Robert Bauman, HHP, June 25, 2013.

37. PNNL, *Hanford and White Bluffs*, 17.

38. Edith King, interview by Ellen Prendergast, PNNL, 24.

39. Robert Fletcher, interview by Robert Bauman, HHP, August 20, 2013.

40. Morris Slavens, interview by Ellen Prendergast, PNNL, 24.

41. Chatters, ed., "History of Cultural Resources Management Activity,"44.

42. Martha Berry Parker, *Tales of Richland, White Bluffs and Hanford, 1805–1943: Before the Atomic Reserve* (Fairfield, WA: Ye Galleon Press, 1986), 61.

43. Meinig, *The Great Columbia Plain*, 69.

44. G. Lindeman and K. Williams, *Resource Protection Planning Process* (RP3)—Agricultural Study Unit (revised by Office of Archaeology and Historic Preservation, Olympia, WA, 1986), 16.

45. PNNL, *Hanford and White Bluffs*, 17.

46. Ibid., 18.

47. Yvonne McGee, interview by Ellen Prendergast, PNNL 2003, 4.

48. PNNL, *Hanford and White Bluffs*, 19.

49. Ibid., 18.

50. Walt Grisham, interview by Ellen Prendergast, PNNL, 18.

51. Slavens interview.

52. Fletcher interview.

53. Bunnell interview.

54. Ibid.

55. Kubik, *Richland*, 21.

56. Chatters, ed., "History of Cultural Resources Management Activity," D.79.

57. Ibid.

58. Ibid.

59. Ibid., D.83.

60. Ibid.

61. Ibid., D.84.

CHAPTER TWO

"We Worked in the Orchards and We Played in the River"

Life in the Towns of Richland, White Bluffs, and Hanford

Robert Franklin

Euro-American settlement came late to the Priest Rapids Valley. Reliable irrigation, needed to farm the sandy but rich soils of the Mid-Columbia, did not materialize until after the 1902 Newlands Reclamation Act funded irrigation projects in the West. Once created, irrigation districts struggled to provide water to farmers due to the sandy soils and high cost of maintenance. The farmers made do. The lucky (or insightful) ones had acreage near the Columbia River, and close to the water table, where they could use wells and pumps to supply their needs. Others packed up and left the dry, dusty landscape; dead trees between rows of dry irrigation furrows and an unpainted shack remained as bleak evidence of their hard work.

Nevertheless, some settlers persisted and developed working farms, ranging in size from the 533-acre Bruggemann Ranch to the five- to twenty-acre farmsteads and soldier settlements. Through trial and error, they found the right crops for the soil and climate. Life was hard on the farm and many had just enough to feed their livestock and family. Fluctuating prices for agricultural goods and the economic downturn of the Great Depression hit rural and urban inhabitants alike, although with access to water and land, rural residents could usually grow enough food for sustenance. This chapter uses the voices of the former residents to illustrate the struggles of farming the Mid-Columbia, the sense of community created in the four-decade life of Hanford and White Bluffs, and community responses to the Great Depression.

How did the agriculturists get there, and why was Euro-American settlement of the Mid-Columbia later than other areas of Washington State? Fur trappers employed by the Hudson's Bay Company (HBC) and the Astorians or Boston Men (working for the American John Jacob Astor) had first explored the area. The HBC constructed an outpost on the Franklin County side of the Columbia directly across from the White Bluffs Landing. Lloyd Wiehl, whose family was among the first settlers in the White Bluffs area, remembers this as an old, unused structure made of driftwood and homemade nails and torn down by the Manhattan Project.[1] Wiehl's maternal grandmother's family, the Craigs, came to the White Bluffs area in 1892 and founded the first school and post office on the Franklin County side of the Columbia.[2] White Bluffs moved across the river to Benton County in the early 1900s, and moved again in the early 1910s to be closer to the railroad.

Before this time, its indigenous inhabitants used the area seasonally, like the Wanapum who fished the river and engaged in cultural ceremonies on Rattlesnake and Gable Mountains. Cattle ranchers and sheepherders ranged their herds over the Mid-Columbia, including the Rattlesnake Hills, Yakima Ridge, and the Cold Creek area beginning in the 1850s. Cattle supplied a vital source of meat for Northwest gold miners and one of the supply routes crossed the White Bluffs ferry landing and continued up the Cariboo Trail to British Columbia or the Frazer Road to the Spokane area and Fort Colville.[3] A series of devastating winters in the 1860s through the 1880s, and the consolidation of the cattle industry, thinned herds and many cattlemen grudgingly gave way to subsistence farmers.

The federal government began building roads in the area (or improving established Indian trails) in the 1850s, connecting army outposts or supplying the Northwest gold strikes in Canada, Idaho, and northwest Washington Territory. Beginning in the 1880s steamers plied the Columbia as far as White Bluffs landing, providing vital communication and market links for the products of the nascent farms. It was not until 1912–1913 that a spur of the Chicago, Milwaukee, and St. Paul snaked down the Columbia to White Bluffs and Hanford. (Richland did not

White Bluffs train station, circa 1944. *Hanford History Project, Harry and Juanita Anderson Collection, RG41_1036.*

get a rail connection until after the evacuation in 1943.) The railroad proved cheaper and more reliable than the river steamers, whose traffic gradually diminished. The railroad spur known as "Sagebrush Annie" travelled south along the river from Beverly, through the whistle-stops of Riverland, Haven, and Allard, and then cut inland about a mile to terminate at the town of Hanford, stopping at the new White Bluffs along the inland curve.

Homesteaders, such as the Craig family, began to arrive in the 1890s and early 1900s, most settling the hills around Rattlesnake Mountain, as much of the land along the river was owned by land developers, the State of Washington, or the federal government. The lone source of surface water in that area, Rattlesnake Spring, was a lifeline to early settlers and many dug ditches from the spring to their fields or, like the Fletcher family who came in 1905, hand-carried water from the spring to their homestead over two miles away. Some families, like the Bennetts and the McGees, drilled wells several hundred feet to the water table below. Dale McGee remembers that in 1928 the well his father Chester drilled reached a depth of 1,150 feet, hit an aquifer with 90 pounds pressure, and flowed over 1,850 gallons a minute, capable of irrigating over 300 acres.[4] As a consequence it dried up the well of Chester's parents, the Browns, on their land in the upper end of the Cold Creek valley. Unlike the basin area below, Cold Creek lacked electricity until after WWII and irrigation was not feasible with diesel or gas pumps. Today the Brown land grows grapes with well water brought up with electric powered pumps.[5]

Like the homesteaders, economic survival for the agriculturalists depended on access to irrigation water. Farmers closer to the river used a patchwork of irrigation styles and engaged in countless battles against erosion and the irrigation companies to keep the water flowing. As mentioned, the size of farms varied in the Priest Rapids Valley from 500 acres to the more common five- to twenty-acre tracts of those who came to farm the area around White Bluffs, Hanford, and Richland. Land developers such as the Hanford Irrigation and Power Company bought large tracts of land and subdivided them. Families looking to escape the city or more marginal farmland during the Great Depression purchased other small plots. The State of Washington gave World War I veterans twenty-acre tracts in the area between Hanford and White Bluffs in an unsuccessful attempt to provide for veterans and develop the state and federal arid lands. The small size of the tracts was understandable as the labor-intensive nature of irrigated fields before mechanization and automation meant that a typical farm family had their hands full with ten or twenty acres.

The history of the irrigation companies in the region is marked with litigation between them and the renters—company against farmer for nonpayment, and farmer against company for failing to keep up with maintenance resulting in weak crop yields or dead crops. Walt Grisham, a former White Bluffs resident, recalls that his father originally settled in an old soldier settlement house and later bought a foreclosed property from the First Bank of White Bluffs. It was a smaller property and the division among crops was common for the area: "We had seven acres of peaches and four acres of apricots, two acres of grapes that we planted, a little patch of asparagus. Like most of the farms in those days, they were small. A lot of the work was done by hand.... You couldn't handle very large farms, unless you went to extra help, which you had to hire help all the time."[6] It was common for irrigators to plant cash crops like asparagus and peppermint in between the rows of fruit trees (or vines) to have a marketable crop in the three to six years it took for fruit-bearing trees to produce.

Those that bought abandoned farmsteads, like the Grishams, skipped the backbreaking first step in agriculture—clearing and leveling the land for planting. An abundance of smooth granite boulders, glacial erratics from the Ice Age floods, littered the land. Settlers employed horse- or later tractor-drawn sagebrush "scrubbers" to clear the land before leveling.[7] In 1920 Robert Fletcher's father bought twenty acres of "all sagebrush.... He had to arrange to get the teams of horses to pull out the sagebrush and level the ground."[8] Scrubbers were the common method of clearing ground, although Madeline Gilles "found a blasting cap that my dad brought from Butte [Montana] to blow up the sagebrush. It was big and tough to make more land, you know. And so, I found an old one, and I thought it was full of dirt, picked at it and it blew up. Took my fingers off. But I made it."[9]

Now cleared of native foliage, the arid land needed reliable delivery of water to transform the dry but rich soils into an irrigated paradise. Early irrigators learned that the Columbia south of Priest Rapids did not have the gradient necessary for a gravity-fed canal that could simply divert water from the river. This explained why the district had remained un-irrigated and undeveloped until the Priest Rapids Irrigation and Power Company (PRIPC), formed in the early 1900s, began construction of a seventeen-mile dirt and concrete canal from the Allard Pump House to the town of Hanford. The genesis of this project came from a Wenatchee businessperson, Manley Bostwick Haynes, who saw the possibilities of orchards in the area and believed he could overcome the technical difficulties that prevented large-scale irrigation. He bought 32,000 acres south of White Bluffs and convinced his well-connected father-in-law, Judge Cornelius Hanford of Seattle, to invest. Disagreements among

"Dad's homestead and sagebrush scrubber invention." *Hanford History Project, Harry and Juanita Anderson Collection, RG41_052.*

investors resulted in the splitting of the PRIPC into two new competing companies: the Hanford Irrigation and Power Company (HIPC) and the White Bluffs Irrigation Company (WBIC). The Allard Pump House, now run by HIPC, used power from the Priest Rapids diversion dam and power plant upriver to raise the water sixty feet from the river to the canal, known as the "Hanford Ditch." Dale McGee recalled a major flaw in the ditch: "they never lined the canal and the canal leaked like a sieve and what happened was it raised the water table through most of the area, [and] many dug wells and irrigated out of them rather than trying to carry water to their places in leaky lateral ditches from the main canal."[10] Furthermore, "that whole area through White Bluffs and Hanford had an extremely high-water table due to this canal. And the moment that they stopped pumping…it started dropping…they were through farming, but the thing that maintained the water table was the canal from Allard."[11] The cost of these irrigation works was substantial and there was intense pressure to recruit as many buyers as possible for HIPC tracts.[12]

The White Bluffs Irrigation Company used a gas-powered pump, the Todd Plant, to supply water via wood stave pipes to the White Bluffs area. A third company was the White Bluffs City and Orchard Tracts (WBCOT) that purchased six hundred acres of old homestead, government, and railroad land near the White Bluffs town site. WBCOT also used a pump and wood stave pipe system to provide water for irrigation and residential/commercial use in White Bluffs. WBIC experienced frequent water delivery problems and the destruction of the Todd Plant in August of 1907 prompted lawsuits by farmers. Growers that could not switch to the WBCOT system hauled water by barrel from the river every evening to pour on their fledgling orchards. Some lost everything and others, sensing the fragility of irrigation farming, left the area while they could. Those that stayed had their contracts switched to HIPC, which continued operations until 1930.

A mixture of irrigation systems and companies spread like patchwork over the Priest Rapids Valley, and although every farmer relied on irrigation, many different types of irrigation systems were in use. Farmers sourced water from the river in the form of pumps or one of the major ditches in the area. Others drilled wells—the aforementioned McGees and others on the plateau drilled hundreds of feet to reach the artesian water. Lateral ditches and pipes ran from the main canal and delivered water to fields. Most homes did not have running water because pumps were used to bring water to the fields before the home—irrigation was always the first priority.

Leatris Reed, whose family came to White Bluffs in 1936, remembers irrigating with well water. "[Y]ou dug the ditch across the field. And then you made little rows out of that on both sides. And you would run it from the well pipe into that big main ditch. And then you would take the little ditches and close them up…. We didn't have running water in the house. We went out and got it by the bucketful off of the well."[13] Many farmers used this type of irrigation, called real, or rill, irrigation. The Johnson family came to the Richland area in 1918 and used rill irrigation from a canal, which was "a concrete pump that run at the head of the field. And it had little holes in it. And then they had cedar plugs that they put in it. And when they wanted the water…, they took that plug out, and away it went."[14]

Walt Grisham's family farm had irrigation water from a canal system consisting of underground wood stave piping that "came up out of the ground and into a weir box. The ditch rider would be able to check the amount of water that you were getting by measuring the amount of water coming over that weir."[15] From the weir the water was distributed by pipe to corrugations for irrigating:

> You would have to put a plug in the pipe to keep the water in. When you wanted to irrigate the particular corrugation, you would pull the plug…the plugs were made out of cedar—we made our own plugs. They were 5–6 inches long. We would sit out on the sunny side of the barn in the wintertime where it was warm and make our plugs. We would whittle off ½ of that plug. If we wanted to regulate the water and not give as much for a particular kind of corrugation… then we would turn the plug around and stick it back in the pipe. By moving that back and forth we could control the water pretty precisely.[16]

Vitrified clay irrigation piping on the Bruggemann homestead is an example of one of the varied types of irrigation systems developed in the Priest Rapids Valley. *Robert Bauman, 2012.*

Robert Fletcher's father lacked a farming background and struggled to build a working irrigation system. His struggles are illustrative of the hard conditions in the arid West and the tenuous relationship between the need for cash income to construct and support the farm, and the work needed to set up the farm in a profitable manner.

It was 1920 and he told me that he had to put in the irrigation. The company brought water to the edge of your property and then you had to put in the pipe yourself. They were cement pipes, about three feet long, 40 pounds, eight inches in diameter. And he said he put in several hundred feet of this pipe and he thought he'd done a pretty good job. He worked hard. Turned the water on and it just leaked all over, so he had to do it all over again. He was pretty persistent. And then they had a hard time the first few years because he was small, a small person, and a greenhorn. About the only income work you could get then was to work for the irrigation company if you wanted to earn some money. And usually that was when the water was shut off and they had to clean and repair the ditches, open ditches. And he said they wouldn't hire him for a year or two because they thought well, he was a greenhorn. He wouldn't last anyway, and he was kind of small. But he stuck it out.[17]

In addition to needing income to support the irrigation system before the crops matured, most if not all, farms depended on cash for staple goods that could not be grown, such as flour, sugar, and coffee. Interviewees recall the reliance on family labor to run all the operations of the farm. Farms at the subsistence level could not afford to hire outside labor and children were a vital source of labor for parents, as well as additional mouths to feed. Walt Grisham recalled the importance of his family's cows:

We didn't sell the milk, we sold the cream. The skim milk was fed to the chickens and the hogs, I had the hog operation. I went next door to the neighbor, who had a dairy, and got his skim milk…and fed it to the chickens and the hogs.[18]

Children worked from an early age, with tasks increasing in complexity and strength over time. It would not do to call these "chores" in the modern sense of the word—children on subsistence farms ran essential aspects of the farm operation. As children, Gordon Kaas and Emma Kleinknecht would wake up before dawn and cut asparagus before the school bus came—they would not get to go to school if they did not finish.[19] LaVerne Sloppy's family had cows that he had to care for. "Well, I started out milking one cow when I was about…six or seven. And I turned a hammer—the separator for the cream, separating the milk and the cream. And…chores in the house…I was carrying water for my mother to wash clothes. Because we didn't have house-water in the house."[20]

Morris Slavens had similar duties to supply the family with basic necessities:

> We had no running water in our home. We had a well and it was one of my jobs to go out and pump several buckets of water to put in the house. We had a bucket by the door with a dipper...we kids just drank it out of the dipper. We had an outhouse, it was about 50 feet away, soon as it filled up, we'd move out another 10 or 15 feet and dig a new hole and move it over. My mother had to cook in those hot Hanford weathers on an iron, cast-iron stove in the middle of 105 degrees. Another job was keeping the wood box filled...we had a pot-bellied stove in the living room and we kept that going and of course it died down during the night, and my mother was always the first one up so she'd start a fire and the rest of us would dress around the stove. But the biggest problem was in laundry and baths...in the winter it was my job to go out to the pump and carry bucket after bucket of water in to fill the boiler on the stove and rise water tubs...I don't really remember taking too many baths.[21]

The Slavens family's story is a common one on rural farmsteads before World War II—most farms in the Priest Rapids Valley lacked indoor plumbing. Crops had priority for water. Only when that need was satisfied would farmers consider any mechanical improvements for the house. It was the same for electricity and appliances. Money went into farm improvements and pumps to deliver the water for the crops before "luxuries" like a refrigerator or washing machine. Walt Grisham draws a clear parallel between the prioritization of effort on the farm to starting a farm today: "If people were to start out from scratch—a piece of bare ground—it would be a big mistake to build a fancy house, with a fancy kitchen, rugs on the floor before the farm. Needs were taken care of. The farm needs to buy the house. You can get by with the basics, but in time, if the farm is successful, it is going to buy the house."[22]

The farmers of the Priest Rapids Valley depended on a complex network of irrigation systems and the regular delivery of water to keep their crops and orchards alive in the arid valley. Those that used their small acreage wisely survived economic downturns and even began to prosper in the years leading up to World War II. Farmers planted crops in between the rows of orchard fruit, changed crops and tree fruits to match market demand, and some began to expand their farms, although too much expansion meant bringing on additional labor. The first tree fruits tried were apples, but in the years before the depression, farmers began to rip out the apple trees and replace them with "soft fruits" such as peaches and apricots. The climate of the Priest Rapids Valley was not conducive to the proper ripening of apples as Dale McGee explains:

> In the 1920s, everybody though that apples were the things to grow in the area, apples and pears. So, they all planted orchards. Well they found out that they couldn't compete with Wenatchee because the apples wouldn't turn color and in those days color had practically everything to do with price…so they would go on the market and they wouldn't be a prime apple…So suddenly they discovered in the late 20s and early 30s that it was just prime country for soft fruit—cherries, apricots and peaches. The people that caught onto this toward the end of the 30s were starting to make money. And these people were just starting to make a real good living when the war broke out, and of course then the Manhattan Project moved in.[23]

The economy of the valley consisted of crops mainly grown for export, although a small amount of fruit and vegetables were canned and consumed locally, and a largely barter or cash economy for staples like coffee, sugar, and flour that could not be grown. Each town had a small mercantile store: the John Dam store in Richland, Reierson's Grocery in White Bluffs, and Boies' store in Hanford. The area also had a creamery, fruit packing warehouses and icehouses for the shipment of tree fruits/soft fruits to outside markets. Mercantile stores of the era were not like those today. Shoppers presented lists and the owner or store clerk retrieved items for them. A common practice was to write up the amount owed by each family and the debt was paid off when the family had some amount of cash, usually after the harvest was sold. Morris Slavens recalled with vivid detail his trips to the store in Hanford:

> That was really [a] remarkable store, I can't imagine the items that [Mr. Boies] had in there, it was so dark and gloomy…I'd go down there and he had high-top button shoes from the 1890s that he couldn't sell and he just kept them, he had horse collars and he had a gasoline pump outside and alongside it a kerosene pump for people that were still using kerosene lamps…People in those days, put it all on a monthly bill, you didn't have much cash, and so they didn't pay cash. For example, my

mother would take my dad's postal check, go over to the store, cash it and pay the bill for the last month, for all the groceries. And for all the groceries purchased, Boies, the owner, would give her a sack of candy for the kids. So every first of the month it was really a great deal to pay that bill and get a sack of candy because you just couldn't raise any money for candy or anything else.[24]

Another practice common to homesteading and truck farming was securing cash income from outside the farm to supply basic needs while the farm was established, or to supplement farm income, especially in meager years. Claude Rawlins's family lived on ten acres of former soldier settlement land and his father worked during the winters for the Utah Idaho Sugar Company plant in Nampa, Idaho, to earn money to supply the production of ten acres, a small farm for the area. Rawlins remembered "[nobody] ever bought food or vegetables from the store. Nobody would do that...we would save [food] in the cellar or something through the winter, or by canning."[25] Yvonne McGee's father sold the cream from his milk cows to the creamery, conveniently located next to the Reierson's Grocery Store in White Bluffs, and used the money for buying basics at the grocery store.[26] Running a successful farm depended on being able to balance several sources of income and sustenance.

Soldier settlements provide a useful example of the challenges in operating a successful farm in the Priest Rapids Valley in the early twentieth century. The effort that created the soldier settlements in the State of Washington has a long and poorly understood history at the state and federal level. Land as payment for military service has a long history in many different cultures in world history. In America, land was part of a military service bonus from the Revolutionary War until just before the Civil War, when the government switched to a cash system for veterans. The Homestead Act of 1862 was part of a political movement to open up land in the West for all citizens, although veterans of the Civil War could deduct the time they served from the five-year residency requirement. Similar requirements existed for World War I vets who wished to take up small plots of land in Washington State as soldier settlements. These settlements were not strictly a program of the federal government, rather a patchwork of state and federal programs that assisted veterans. Soldier settlements were often on state or federal land.[27] A nationwide program under the Interior Department during the Wilson administration, led by Franklin K. Lane to assist World War I veterans with farmable land, failed to gain traction due to opposition by commercial farmers, the USDA, and the National Grange, and it was left to individual states to provide land assistance.[28] In the soldier settlements near Hanford and White Bluffs, each soldier received a one-bedroom house, a well, pump, and outbuilding (usually a garage) and some basic farming equipment on terms of repayment. There was no requirement of previous farming experience to receive a soldier settlement.

The program in Washington State located in Hanford and White Bluffs, run by the Washington State Department of Veterans Affairs, provided resident veterans a cash or land "Veterans' Bonus" under the Veterans' Equalized Compensation Act.[29] This veteran's assistance was part of a larger effort to head off a labor surplus caused by the return of 1.5 million World War I veterans. Planners believed that veterans should not be given homesteads, rather they were to be paid wages and apply their savings to a down payment for a homestead, or receive advance money for a homestead and improvements to be repaid over a period of time. City-bred soldiers with little to no farm experience were to work on reclamation projects to gain valuable farm experience.[30] Two competing concerns, one of modern industrial economic anxiety and the other rooted in wistful romanticism of yeoman farming, rise to the forefront in this and other "back-to-the-land" movements in the first few decades of the twentieth century. The desire to stimulate postwar industrial consumption and avoid large numbers of unemployed veterans in urban areas reflected the first concern. This motive recognized markers of a functioning and healthy modern economy—low unemployment and discretionary spending. The second addressed the shift of the American population toward the city.[31] Proponents of "back-to-the-land" colony settlement schemes wanted to increase the portion of land-owning citizens to foster patriotism and Americanization, and create model communities free from what progressive reformers saw as the worst parts of urban life—overcrowding, disease, poverty, and diversity of ethnic languages and backgrounds. Nostalgia for the farm was a common virus that infected the "back-to-the-land" movement and soldier settlements.[32]

The marketing of farming land in Hanford and White Bluffs by the "Hanford Bunch" and other investors in the various irrigation companies, and the ability of state governments in the western United States to colonize arid lands with veterans, shared similar obstacles. By the turn of the twentieth century, the desire for homesteads and subsistence farming was declining for several reasons. First, a rapidly industrializing economy needed wage earners, and the gradual mechanization of agriculture and introduction of cheap fertilizer meant farmers could work more land, (and more productive land) with less labor. These push and pull factors meant that the demand for industrial and urban workers was increasing as opportunities in rural areas were declining. Second, the rise of the market economy and desire for consumer goods created a dissatisfaction with rural life and the economic and social limitations of subsistence level farming. Many Americans wanted to take advantage of new advancements like refrigeration, automobiles, radios, and other consumer goods. For many farmers across America, conditions in rural areas in the 1930s often resembled that of a century earlier. To put it simply—farmers wanted to make money and reap the benefits of an industrialized society. And third, much of the productive land in western states suitable for agriculture was already taken, leaving mostly arid lands where agriculture was impossible without irrigation works. The formation of the Bureau of Reclamation in 1902 attempted to solve the problem by creating irrigation districts and reliable water to "unlock" arid lands for irrigation. Many early projects were plagued with insufficient planning, poor site selection, and an unreliable delivery of water. Gradual technological improvements in irrigation and the construction of dams and reservoirs on several of the major rivers in the arid West helped mitigate this issue, including Grand Coulee Dam in central Washington, which irrigates much of the land in the bend of the Columbia River.[33] However, as mentioned earlier in this chapter, problems with the irrigation system plagued farmers in the Priest Rapids Valley, most of whom were operating at a near subsistence level. These same problems—unreliable irrigation, extreme weather, market fluctuations—combined with the inexperience of many of the veterans selected for the soldier settlements, led to high levels of abandonment of the settlements and the program's eventual termination in the mid-1920s.

Several of the Priest Rapids Valley residents knew of the soldier settlement program and its impact on the built environment at Hanford and White Bluffs. Yvonne McGee's father received a twenty-acre soldier settlement with a one-bedroom house as a World War I veteran in 1922. He worked off the farm for income and eventually purchased a neighboring tract, renting out his original settlement.[34] His is one of the few success stories, likely due to off-farm cash income. Walt Grisham's family moved to White Bluffs from Yakima to manage two orchards, one for an absentee soldier settler, and Walt grew up in the soldier settlement house. "These were kind of cookie-cutter type houses that were built on each of the farms that were made available for each of the World War I veterans. They had a house, barn, chicken house, and so forth. They were small houses, but they were a roof, and that was about it."[35] For Morris Slavens the soldier settlement houses were enviable, but not the location:

> They were beautiful homes built out on the sagebrush, and they had cisterns for water and so on but nobody ever came, the reason being one, that they didn't give them enough land, and two—the land was all sandy, so they really couldn't raise crops and so those houses just went into disrepair. And when I was a kid, we used to go out there and just walk through them and they were far better houses than what we lived in when they were built.[36]

The abandonment of the soldier settlements was not permanent. The land and buildings were marketed to Mormon families that came from Cache Valley in northern Utah and southeast Idaho. Claude Rawlins recalls his mother being happy with the house, and he offers insight as to the failure of the "back-to-the-land" movement: "I think they found out that 9 out of 10 soldiers were not very good farmers. It takes kind of a special culture to come in and make that work. Everybody works and money doesn't count for very much."[37] Indeed the dissatisfaction with subsistence agriculture and the pressure to pay back farm loans combined to ruin many communitarian agriculture projects in the 1920s and 1930s.

White Bluffs, Hanford, and Richland were small towns centered on agricultural commerce; nevertheless, there were differences between those with cash jobs and those who relied on farming for subsistence.

Interviewees recall the practice of "neighbor exchange," where neighbors would trade labor and share machinery back and forth during relatively lull periods on the farm.[38] Farm families tended to "look up at" the town residents who earned money from steady jobs.[39] Even within the ranks of farmers, there were divisions between prosperous and subsistence-level farmers, between those with orchards and those with ground crops. Most, if not all, farmers grew a diversity of crops, some for home consumption and others for export. These diversified farms are known as "truck farms" or market gardens.[40] Robert Fletcher's farm type "was truck farming. We had to raise—we had to have cows. Truck farming was not too reliable. You had to fall back on a herd of cows—most all farmers had a herd of cattle which they had milk cows and some beef cows."[41] Norman Johnson's family grew asparagus, strawberries, and alfalfa on twenty-seven acres. "My grandpa said that the only people that made any money out of their farming and amount to anything was the ones that had orchards. And [I] asked him how come he didn't plant trees, and he said he couldn't afford to buy any. So, I guess he never made a lot of money."[42]

Each of the three towns had cultural institutions in addition to the commercial cores. Each town had a grade and high school (some housed in the same building), a Grange Hall, and several denominations of churches. White Bluffs boasted Pop English's drugstore that served ice cream, a common remembrance among interviewees who visited as children; a movie theater run by Edmund Anderson that had weekly showings; and the *White Bluffs Spokesman,* a weekly newspaper. In addition, interviewees recall community events such as dances, sports, the Priest Rapids Band, holiday celebrations, and informal gatherings that often consisted of swimming in the Columbia River or in the irrigation ditches.

Interviewees proudly remembered their schooling, perhaps because it was a respite from the rigors of farm work. Lloyd Wiehl's family was one of the first to the White Bluffs area and his grandmother formed the first school and held classes in a one-room log cabin first on the east side of the Columbia River in Franklin County, and then later on the west side in Benton County. A grade school sufficed until Lloyd was of high school age, when his father Matt led the push for an accredited high school.

[My] dad got to work again he bought a house on the west side of the river where the town was, so he called his residence there in Benton County. He ran for school board and was elected chairman of the school board. So, then he went to Seattle [and] hired some school teachers so they could be accredited. Two of them were Phi Beta Kappas, one of whom was Mary Powell [Harris] who wrote the book *Goodbye, White Bluffs*.[43]

White Bluffs resident Leatris Reed remembers that the grade school "did not have separate rooms [for grades 1–3], but we had little partitions that she [teacher Alice Moody] would put up so that we would keep our attention."[44] Reed stated that the children were largely self-policing both in the classroom and in the playground due to the small class sizes and close-knit community.

At Hanford, seven miles south of White Bluffs, schooling was an important part of the community as well. The Hanford High School, built in 1916 and one of the few remaining pre-Manhattan Project structures on the Hanford Site, was considered the pride and joy of the community and apparently served grades one through twelve. Rod Bunnell remembers that the Hanford school burned around Christmas of 1936 and the students had to make alternate arrangements. The grade school moved temporarily to the Planters Hotel in Hanford and the high school students were sent to White Bluffs. In the hotel, primary grades were in the lobby, grades four through six were in the dining room, and grades seven and eight were in the kitchen.[45] A year later, the grade school moved to the community hall. Some in the two communities worried about whether the high school students could get along—a friendly rivalry had developed between the two schools large enough to have high school sports teams in the Priest Rapids Valley. Walt Grisham explained, "We were almost bitter enemies trying to get along in the same building. Well it took about 3 or 4 days, and everything was just great. We fielded an outstanding basketball team."[46] Several years later, the White Bluffs High School burned down and those students were sent to the newly rebuilt Hanford High School.

Between Hanford and Richland was the small community of Fruitvale, now northern Richland. Emma Kleinknecht went to grade school in the

Fruitvale School, which also served as a church, dance hall, and Grange Hall for the residents. In Richland, Robert Fletcher attended Lewis and Clark grade school for grades one through eight. Each grade had its own room, each room heated by a coal-burning stove. Restrooms were outside. Fletcher recalls his pleasure at attending Richland High School with its indoor restrooms. Students that lived close enough could walk to school.

Hanford High School before eviction. *Hanford History Project, Harry and Juanita Anderson Collection, RG41_1264.*

Hanford High School in July 2017. *Robert Franklin.*

Bus service existed for those who lived far enough to need it. The school district chartered a farmer to build a bus, usually a converted truck bed with seats and a canvas roof. Manufactured busses did not come to the area until just before World War II.

Church was another staple of life in rural America, and the Priest Rapids Valley had most of the major Christian denominations—Methodist, Presbyterian, and Catholic. A noteworthy religious development in the region was the arrival of twenty to thirty Mormon families in 1939. This

"White Bluffs School Bus, Driven by Edmund Anderson." *Hanford History Project, Harry and Juanita Anderson Collection, RG41_175.*

migration resulted in one of the largest Mormon communities in the rural Northwest. These families had been marketed old soldier settlement land that had defaulted back to the owners, and many plots came with a house, well, and crop in the ground. The real estate brokers especially marketed to Mormons because of the reputation they had as farmers with large families, a strong work ethic, and knowledge of irrigation and arid lands.[47] The Mormons never established their own meeting house in the Priest Rapids Valley; rather they met in the Grange Hall at

White Bluffs. Mormonism was gaining a gradual acceptance in American society in the 1930s and 1940s as population pressures in Utah forced many Mormons to strike out for more robust economies in West Coast population centers.[48] In these new communities, Mormons pursued a policy of "Americanization" and joined secular social and community organizations such as the Boy Scouts. In addition, Mormon participation in the armed services in World Wars I and II further integrated Mormons into the American mainstream. Many migrants, however, remembered the persecution of their ancestors in the nineteenth century. Claude Rawlins, who came as a small child in 1939 remembers the fears his mother had about leaving Utah:

> She was very angry with my father, for trying to take us away from Utah and bring us out here. She said that [many] people said, "boy when you go out there away from the church they are not going to treat you like they do back home." Then she kind of had to repent to him, my father (and she did), that this was the most friendly inviting place she had ever been to in her life. She loved the people that were there and the people loved the group of Mormons. She said she had never lived in such a loving, warm community in her whole life.[49]

Many of the non-Mormon interviewees who specifically mention the arrival of the Mormons just four years before the evacuation shared these feelings of affection and acceptance. The closeness between the religious communities and lack of prejudice reflects the interdependence of neighbors in the tiny and close-knit community and the changing status of Mormons in American life.

The Grange, or the National Grange of the Order of Patrons of Husbandry, was another facet of rural life and culture that enjoyed popularity from its founding shortly after the Civil War. Formally an agricultural advocacy group, the Grange Hall was a fixture in most small, rural communities and an all-purpose facility that often held dances, religious ceremonies (like those of the transplanted Mormons), school events, and other public functions. Madeline Gilles recalls going to the Richland Grange with her parents for meetings and dances, where her mother would play piano for the dances and drill team.[50] The economic situation of subsistence farmers in the Great Depression and afterward did not curtail the dances—it often just forced attendees to be more efficient with the material available for dresses. Growing up in White Bluffs, Shirley Buckman made new dresses in a community that did not have a clothing store. "The parents took us all to the dances and some of us girls…we would run to town and get a flour sack and make us a new skirt and a blouse and away we'd go."[51] What is now considered "do it yourself" was then a necessity of rural life.

"Swimmers posing for picture at the Wiehl Ranch," date unknown. *Hanford History Project, Harry and Juanita Anderson Collection, RG4I_131.*

Perhaps the source of recreation and community life most fondly remembered by interviewees was the Columbia River. Multiple interviewees recalled swimming in the Columbia during hot days, or in the irrigation ditch if they were not allowed in the river (perhaps because of the current). It is likely that this frequency is more due to the youth of the interviewees; parents would have had fewer opportunities for recreation than children. Leatris Reed summed up best the intense feelings that interviewees had for the river and its importance to their childhoods:

Oh, the river. The river was a godsend. We learned to swim the first year, the first summer we were there. And we had a raft…[a]nd if you could swim out to the raft—I was not supposed to, but I did. And the little Lowe boy wasn't supposed to, either. He was just learning how to swim. And he went under. And my sister Dorothy was a really good swimmer...[a]nd she went down and got him, got him out on that—pulled him up. And there was a couple of guys up there that pulled him up on that raft and they turned him over on his stomach. And the water just poured. And he lived. And every one of those kids at White Bluffs were just as devoted as that to the river. That was our playground. We had to do our work in the morning because it was cool enough. And the summers over there were—boy they were hot. But we could go in and get in the swimming pool then, our swimming pool.[52]

In the winter when the Columbia River froze over, ice skating was a common diversion, as was gathering ice for iceboxes. Shirley Buckman remembers, "if somebody decided that we were going to go ice-skating or something, they would call up and say, bring a dish, we are going to have a picnic down at the river and skate."[53] Former White Bluffs resident Walt Grisham talked about the meaning of the Columbia to the community. "We always refer to it as 'our river.' My Dad used to say, because we spent some time in California...he said boy, if California had this river down there, they would put a fence around it and charge to see it."[54]

The sandy sagebrush environment did pose a threat to early automobiles, and provided a home for the jackrabbits that threatened ground crops. A common community effort of the arid West was the rabbit drive, where the entire community would gather and drive jackrabbits into a corral or natural feature where they were exterminated. Madeline Gilles remembered: "they used to have rabbit drives. A lot of men would get together so far apart and they'd drive the rabbits in front of them and then shoot them because they were a real menace. They'd get into your garden and eat everything up."[55] The communities of Hanford, White Bluffs, and Richland clearly centered on farming and the institutions of rural life—school, church, the Grange, and the natural environment where they were situated.

The Great Depression is perhaps the defining international event, prior to World War II, that residents of the Priest Rapids Valley experienced. Interviewees recalled the hard times that accompanied economic strangulation and stagnation, but tempering those memories was a sense of community and an attitude of survivability.

"Rabbit Drive at White Bluffs," date unknown.
Hanford History Project, Harry and Juanita
Anderson Collection, RG41_262.

Edith King grew up in Hanford, and she asserted that those with farms did not really suffer because they could grow their own food. However, her father lost his job at the irrigation company office and could only find employment as a "ditch-walker," someone who walks along the irrigation ditch looking for problems. However, the struggling company could not pay him cash so he was paid in script; "they are just a piece of paper worth whatever he would get, but you couldn't cash them. They had to hold them. Well, eventually you would get something out of them and when he finally did, he only got a percentage of that money. He never got the full amount."[56]

Other interviewees recall a more troubling time; even surrounded by orchards many suffered and some lost everything as falling agricultural prices left orchardists with unmarketable crops. Morris Slavens grew up in Hanford from 1922 until he left at age fifteen in 1937. His father owned a small plot, five acres, and planted apples "border to border." By 1929 he had "made quite a bit of money on it." The Depression put an end to his orchard.

> [H]e continued to try and raise apples but it was a losing game. He borrowed money on his insurance, he borrowed money from my mother's sister, and one year I recall, it cost him five cents a box to market those apples. And he just couldn't make it. He just kept hoping that we'd come out of the depression but we didn't do it. Other growers were in the same

position and things got so bad that they would dump the apples in the old rock crusher holes and they also dumped them in the river. I recall going down to the Columbia and seeing that the water was just red with apples floating down the river because they couldn't get rid of them.[57]

Gordon Kaas, who grew up in Richland, remembers that his father also had an apple orchard but during the Depression "apples was one thing that people didn't have to have and consequently, the market went away."[58] His father decided to bulldoze the apple trees and planted peppermint, which they grew until eviction in 1943.

During many of the oral histories conducted over the years with former Hanford and White Bluffs residents, interviewees were asked to reflect on the community they called home. A few had less than fond memories. Morris Slavens, who left Hanford in 1937, had no love lost for the Priest Rapids Valley, saying "after I left Hanford, I was really happy to get out of that hot, you know, Godforsaken place, I really was." In regards to the life of the community, though, most were wistful and reflective about their lives in the Priest Rapids Valley. To Walt Grisham, "White Bluffs was a great place to grow up. It was something—the river was there, we worked in the orchards and we played in the river…it was kind of like an oasis in the desert."[59]

Notes

1. Judge Lloyd Wiehl, interview by Ellen Prendergast, Hanford Cultural Resources Laboratory (HCRL), August 23, 2000. The HBC structure is often confused with a later structure, still standing on the Franklin County side, used as a barracks and blacksmith shop.

2. Ibid.

3. For more information see Ron Anglin, *Forgotten Trails: Historical Sources of the Columbia's Big Bend Country* (Pullman: Washington State University Press, 1995).

4. Dale G. McGee, interview by Ellen Prendergast, HCRL, July 11, 2001.

5. The Federal Government condemned the Fletcher, McGee, and other farmsteads on the east slope of Rattlesnake Mountain and the Rattlesnake Hills for the Manhattan Project in 1943. Used as a buffer zone for the Hanford Site, along with the Wahluke Slope north of the Columbia River, they were later returned to the public domain as the Hanford Reach, the Arid Lands Ecology Preserve, or sold to private individuals for farming.

6. Walter W. Grisham, interview by Robert Bauman, HCRL, September 20, 2000.

7. On the Hanford Site today there is evidence that at least one enterprising farmer used the glacial erratics as a building material. The structures commonly known as the Bruggemann Warehouse and Cookhouse are constructed of these glacial erratics embedded in

concrete and are the first stop on the Pre-Manhattan Project tour run by the Manhattan Project National Historical Park. A house of similar construction once existed on the site. Bruggemann did not construct these buildings himself; they were built by the original owner, Von Herberg (first name unknown).

8. Robert Fletcher, interview by Robert Bauman, Hanford Oral History Project (HHP), August 20, 2013.

9. Madeline Gilles, interview by Robert Bauman, HHP, July 2, 2013.

10. Dale G. McGee interview.

11. Ibid.

12. Much of this paragraph comes from *2017 Pre-Manhattan Historic Site Tour Docent Narrative*. Manhattan Project National Historical Park. March 1, 2017.

13. Leatris Reed, interview by Robert Bauman, HHP, August 27, 2013.

14. Norman Johnson, interview by Robert Bauman, HHP, November 5, 2013.

15. Grisham interview.

16. Ibid.

17. Robert Fletcher, interview by Robert Bauman, HHP, August 20, 2013.

18. Grisham interview.

19. Gordon Kaas, interview by Robert Bauman, HHP, June 12, 2013; Kleinknecht interview.

20. LaVerne Sloppy, interview by Robert Bauman, HHP, November 18, 2013.

21. Morris R. Slavens, interview by Ellen Prendergast, HCRL, August 21, 2002.

22. Grisham interview.

23. Dale G. McGee interview.

24. Slavens interview.

25. Claude Rawlins, interview by Ellen Prendergast, HCRL, July 24, 2002.

26. Yvonne McGee, interview by Ellen Prendergast, HCRL, July 11, 2001.

27. Federal programs to aid veterans before 1930 included the Veterans Bureau, the Bureau of Pensions of the Interior Department, and the National Home for Disabled Volunteer Soldiers. In 1930 the three federal programs were consolidated into what eventually became the Veterans Administration.

28. See Bill G. Reid, "Franklin K. Lane's Idea for Veterans' Colonization, 1918–1921," *Pacific Historical Review* 33, no. 4 (1964): 447–61.

29. Veterans Affairs, Department of, World War I Service Statement Cards, 1917–1919, Washington State Archives, Digital Archives, digitalarchives.wa.gov, November 29, 2017.

30. Reid, "Veterans' Colonization."

31. U.S. Department of the Interior, *Annual Report*, (1918), 6.

32. Reid, "Veterans' Colonization," 454.

33. Other dams and irrigation projects near the Hanford Site are the Wanapum and Priest Rapids dams, both of which are run by the Grant County Public Utilities District.

34. Yvonne McGee interview.

35. Grisham interview.

36. Slavens interview.

37. Rawlins interview.

38. Alene Clarke, Shirley Buckman, and Walt Grisham, interview by Ellen Prendergast, HCRL, August 6, 2001.

39. Ibid.

40. "Truck" refers not to the method of transportation but from the old French word *troquer*, meaning "barter" or "exchange."

41. Fletcher interview.

42. Norman Johnson interview.

43. Wiehl interview.

44. Reed interview.

45. Rod Bunnell, interview by Ellen Prendergast, HCRL, July 19, 2001.

46. Grisham interview.

47. Rawlins interview.

48. Todd Forsyth Carney, "Utah and Mormon Migration in the Twentieth Century: 1890–1955," (master thesis, Utah State University, 1992), digital commons.usu.edu/ctd/2061.

49. Rawlins interview.

50. Gilles interview.

51. Shirley Buckman, interview by Ellen Prendergast, HCRL, September 18, 2000. See chapter 3 for more on women in the Grange.

52. Reed interview.

53. Buckman interview.

54. Clarke, Buckman, and Grisham interview.

55. Gilles interview.

56. Edith King, interview by Ellen Prendergast, HCRL, August 20, 2002.

57. Slavens interview.

58. Kaas interview.

59. Grisham interview; Slavens interview.

CHAPTER THREE

Orchards and Open Arms

Women in the Priest Rapids Valley

Laura Arata

A seemingly bleak setting greeted new arrivals to a remote corner of the eastern Washington desert. Looking across the windswept, arid landscape, few realized that the conditions which had brought them to the area in the early years of World War II—vast, open spaces, an abundant supply of water, and access to railroads—were the same ones that had drawn hopeful settlers for nearly a century. Where new arrivals saw empty vistas necessary for shielding a component of the top-secret Manhattan Project, pre-war residents of the Priest Rapids Valley along the Columbia River, which included the communities of Hanford, White Bluffs, and Richland, saw promising and productive farmland, waiting for fruit trees and alfalfa to take root. Male-dominated accounts have long been the most visible records of settlement, but there were hundreds of women among those who labored to transform the area from a sagebrush desert into thriving orchards and fields. While traditional narratives have tended to limit them to roles as the mothers, wives, sisters, and daughters of the men who settled the Priest Rapids Valley, women were active participants. They mediated encounters with Native Americans, maintained home-steads, farmland, and families, and engaged in building the communities of Hanford, White Bluffs, and Richland. Some owned land or businesses independently, and a few moved there alone. And they were devastated to leave when forced by wartime mandates.

Settlement of the Priest Rapids Valley roughly followed broad trends in western American history, and as a result the stories of women remained severely understudied until nearly the end of the twentieth century. Long before the frontier was declared closed in 1890, it was nearly always cast as a masculine space populated by fur traders, miners, cattlemen, farmers, and later the titans of industries like logging and railroads. There was little room for women in the history of the frontier, some argued, because women did not do the work of settling the West. As one writer summarized, though there were approximately 186,930 adult women in the western states and territories by the time of the 1870 census, these women "did not lead expeditions, command troops, build railroads, drive cattle, ride Pony Express, find gold, amass great wealth, get elected to high public office, rob stages, or lead lynch mobs," and therefore did not seem to warrant extensive consideration by historians.[1] This historical marginalization of women continued well beyond World War II, and thus the earliest accounts of pre-war residents of the Priest Rapids Valley tended to sideline the experiences of women. It would be several more decades before historians began to re-envision the West as a multicultural region and acknowledge the contributions of women.[2] As a result, many of the stories collected through the Hanford History Project reflect the unique voices of women in the narrative of the pre-war Priest Rapids Valley communities for the first time. Their recollections help to fill in persistent silences in the historical record.

The first non-Native arrivals in the area were European fur traders, who brought with them Native wives and Métis children.[3] Arriving in the late eighteenth century, their presence energized settlement from the newly independent United States, seeking to gain a foothold in the Pacific Northwest. As a result, the first white woman to enter what became Washington Territory from east of the Mississippi, missionary Narcissa Whitman, reached Walla Walla, just a hundred miles from the Priest Rapids Valley, in 1836. By the 1860s, a fresh generation of pioneer women arrived to usher in the birth of towns that came to be known as White Bluffs, Hanford, and Richland.[4] Women were present and active participants in the settlement of the area for the next eighty years, working alongside husbands, fathers, and brothers, and experiencing life in the West on their own terms. Their experiences mirror patterns seen throughout the West. Following the deaths of Marcus and Narcissa Whitman in the fall of 1847, white settlement was effectively curtailed until a few tentatively moved into the region in 1861. Women were among these earliest arrivals, and would participate in every successive wave of settlement into the following century. While the first written histories of the area tended toward contextualizing the experiences of men, women's recollections make clear that, after enduring hardships similar to those of their more famous counterparts on the Oregon Trail and frontier settlements of the Far West, they viewed their experience in the context of having been true pioneers.

The Homestead Act of 1862 made it possible for prospective settlers to claim up to 160 acres for the nominal sum of $14 for application and filing fees. Women were critical partners in these ventures because each spouse was entitled to make a claim, and thus a husband and wife could together file for 320 acres.[5] As the earliest successful ventures included livestock raising—particularly cattle—additional acreage was a decided advantage. Women in the sparsely settled region faced tremendous isolation and loneliness in the years before convenient travel was possible along the White Bluffs or Wallula-Okanagan roads, and were forced to wait upon a new century to arrive before the railroad finally linked the area to the Yakima Valley. The railroad proved a final link in the chain of necessities for transforming the area into a productive agricultural center. Already blessed with good soil and water, the arrival of the railroad opened the area to larger markets for produce. With this convergence of conditions, settlers transformed thousands of acres of desert land into vineyards, alfalfa fields, and the extensive orchards that would come to characterize White Bluffs in particular.

Early relations with Native people were often mediated by the Hudson's Bay Company, which maintained a presence as early as the 1830s in the area that became known as White Bluffs for its chalky-colored cliffs. An increase in settlement naturally meant additional interaction, and mediating such encounters often fell to women, who maintained homesteads while "men were away from their families for many days at a time herding cattle, driving cattle to market, or working for some other cattlemen in order to earn money or cattle for their own herds." Such was the case with Bill Parker, who brought his wife and children to White Bluffs in 1872 and operated a store and trading post where "Indians came to trade their furs and skins for things they needed."[6] Keeping the trading post stocked and the family supplied often required Bill Parker to leave his wife in charge. In a fitting statement on the privileging of men's experiences over those of women, the first name of Mrs. Parker is not found in any of the early histories of the area.[7]

What befell the family speaks to the often fragile nature of these communities in their first years, and the losses endured by women who assumed primary responsibility for keeping homesteads and families together in the face of great hardships. Mrs. Parker found herself alone with the children one day when "a band of Indian warriors appeared riding along the top of the Bluff upriver from the trail to the settlement." Fearing the Indians might attack the trading post if they knew only women and children were present, she "went reluctantly to meet and talk to them," hoping to indicate that the men would return shortly.[8] As it turned out, the Indians gave her no trouble, but soon after the family suffered a series of tragedies all too common for the time period. In the fall of 1875, Bill Parker set out for The Dalles in search of help for a rapidly growing tumor. Shortly after his departure, the Parker children fell suddenly ill and the two youngest died. Mrs. Parker took her two living daughters to Yakima, where friends took them in. Days later, Bill Parker died.[9] Mrs. Parker, one of the earliest white women to live in the area, never returned to White Bluffs, but her time there had already helped to open the way for further settlement.

Encounters with Native people remained fairly common many years later, and most were friendly. By the late nineteenth century, with the communities of the Priest Rapids Valley well-established, these interactions sometimes took on a new dynamic. Women continued to serve as important mediators, assisting local Indians with tasks like letter writing and taking advantage of the opportunity to learn Native techniques for things such as food preservation from Indian women. Such interactions remained common as late as the 1940s. Murrel Dawson, whose father moved his family to White Bluffs in 1941 in search of work, recalled a local chief, Johnny Buck, who "would come down to our house from time to time," and on some of those visits would sit and converse with Dawson's mother while she wrote letters for him.[10] Leatris Reed recalled that her mother learned to dry fruit from Deloria, one of the wives of Buck's brother, Frank. Noting that the Indians would appear twice a year to fish and gather fruit to dry, Reed remembered them as "fine people" who had friendly relations with their white neighbors, including her own mother. "They would dry fruit all summer long—peaches, cherries, apricot, apples, everything. And they taught my mother that if you soak them just a few minutes in saltwater, they will not turn brown. And they won't salt the fruit. And so, she learned how to do that."[11]

The idea of threatening Natives remained common in sentiment, if not applied to the actual Indians with whom most women interacted. Madeline Gilles recalled several bands of Wanapum Indians camping at the river near her family's ten-acre farm near Richland, and that "my mother used to say to my little sister, 'Rosie, if you don't be good, I'm going to give you to the Indians!'"[12] In reality, as Dawson and Reed's recollections make clear, women's interactions with local Native people appear more often than not to have been friendly and reciprocal in nature. Women were more likely to view daytime visits by local Indian women as a welcome interlude to other chores, and for many who were adjusting to a new kind of life in an unfamiliar location, Indian women possessed knowledge that made essential tasks such as food preservation easier. Both Indian and white women, in other words, served as important mediators as settlement to the area increased.

After decades of a slow but steady increase in white settlement, promises of improved irrigation and land with guaranteed water rights led to a new rush of development. Private land companies "hoping to recreate the speculation bonanza of the late 1880s" began to issue colorful brochures that "reached the West Coast cities and towns, now filled with sawmills and fish canneries, mud and smoke," and tapped into the desires of many to try a different way of life.[13] Women expressed great interest in the opportunities that awaited there, and their opinions and willingness to go were often a critical factor in deciding to relocate. Such was the case for Jeanie Wheeler and her husband Frank, who formed a partnership with her parents in order to move to White Bluffs in 1907. Following the death of an infant during a whooping cough epidemic in the winter of 1906, Frank and Jeanie became convinced that the desert climate would be "more healthy for children" and an improvement over polluted Tacoma where Frank sometimes struggled to find work as a brick mason.[14]

The enthusiasm of Jeanie and her mother, Jane Shaw, was intrinsic to the family's decision to move to White Bluffs, and it was Jane who served as the "critical link" in the family's success. Unlike son-in-law Frank and her own husband, George, Jane "was the one with serious commercial farming experience as a young woman on her parents' farm in Wisconsin" and the energy and organizational skill to ensure the family's success as farmers.[15] Thus it was women like Jane and Jeanie who provided the support, encouragement, and in many cases the knowledge that accompanied farmers to White Bluffs early in the twentieth century. The Shaw and Wheeler families became part of a new wave of settlers determined to transform the area from a desert valley with an abundant water supply into a productive agricultural community. Women's efforts proved essential to the ultimate success of these ventures.

By 1908, driven by land speculation and promises of improved irrigation on the horizon, settlement in Priest Rapids Valley, and especially White Bluffs, had begun to increase. Advertisements peppered newspapers across Washington, proclaiming "Facts that Prove WHY YOU SHOULD INVEST in White Bluffs." Among the lures for prospective settlers were claims that White Bluffs possessed "the best land for the least money in Washington" and that land came with "easy terms; one-fifth down, balance in four equal annual payments, 7 per cent interest, enabling anyone to secure a home."[16] Significantly, women took part in these land transactions independently. While women had been able to independently claim land under the terms of the 1862 Homestead Act, provided they were "at least twenty-one years old, single, widowed, divorced, or head of a household," their ownership of such lands has traditionally been overlooked and understudied. The reality that women were among purchasers of land in the Priest Rapids Valley is in keeping with a larger trend of women's land ownership in the West.[17]

The advertisement mentioned above proclaimed that more than $75,000 worth of land had been sold in just eight days. Among names appearing on an included list of new property owners were several women who had independently purchased property: Dora M. Athow purchased 3.35 acres, while Fanny W. Scott, Mrs. F. Ball, and Ella Wooley each purchased ten. The first three women were all from Washington—Athow from White Bluffs, Scott from North Yakima, and Ball from Tacoma. Ella

Wooley came from London, England, apparently willing and intrepid enough to relocate across an ocean. Her decision indicates that the American West was viewed as a place where opportunities existed for women to own their own land and businesses.

Beyond having property available for purchase, White Bluffs did its best to market itself as a modern and growing community with a number of established and planned businesses. Proudly listing "enterprises permanently established," the advertisement named more than a dozen businesses, including a newspaper, hotel, mercantile, jewelry store, bank, meat market, two doctors, a drugstore, and a post office. Projected enterprises included a store, valued at $2,500, to be opened by Mrs. Churchill, indicating at least some additional opportunity for women to become business owners. Women's ownership of small businesses was, like land ownership, in keeping with larger trends in the American West, where upwards of 80 percent of businesses were independently owned, and where women often found space as entrepreneurs engaged in businesses such as clothing and dressmaking, stationary stores, or restaurants.[18]

By 1913, prospects for growth in the Priest Rapids Valley appeared even brighter, as the journey had been reduced to less than a day's train travel from the metropolitan centers of Portland, Seattle, or Spokane. In response to the arrival of the railroad and construction of a new railway station, the town center of White Bluffs relocated for the third time.[19] Jeanie Wheeler viewed the new train, nicknamed "Sagebrush Annie," as "a godsend," providing an opportunity to visit her girlhood home.[20] To promote the Priest Rapids Line, the railroad issued colorful brochures, filled with information, to stations around the country, which in turn attracted even more new settlers. The arrival of improved rail service sparked yet another burst of growth, building on the farming activity that had begun in earnest in the 1890s. Prospective settlers, lured by promises of abundant water and land for cash crops such as alfalfa, apples, and asparagus, began descending on the valley from all over the country. The valley would continue to grow as a center of agricultural production through the first three decades of the twentieth century.

Many prospective settlers sought exactly that, and for many it represented a chance to start a new life, just as it did for Jeanie and Frank Wheeler. Developing farms was still hard work, but in the Priest Rapids

Valley it became a family affair. The experiences of settlers consistently demonstrate that women did not simply live on the land—they physically worked on it also. Madeline Gilles, whose Croatian-immigrant father left a hard life of mining in Montana in favor of becoming a Washington farmer, recalled that during her childhood the family "had alfalfa and a big garden and strawberries and grapes and raspberries. So, we were busy."[21] Gilles further recalled a life that revolved around seasons and crops: her father planted them, the children helped pick them, and her mother canned

Women and girls commonly worked in the orchards in White Bluffs and Hanford. *Harry Anderson Collection, East Benton County Historical Society, 2008.058.10.*

everything from fruit to sauerkraut, harvested potatoes and turnips, and packed asparagus and strawberries for market. "We picked strawberries. We picked apples. We picked pears. We did those kinds of things for other people, plus we picked our own fruit so our mother could can them," Gilles explained, defining her childhood as "busy," because the children "had to bring the cows from the pasture home in the morning after cutting asparagus—about 3:00 in the morning, you get up, cut asparagus, bring the cows home and milk them and take them back. Get ready for school. It was busy."[22] In other words, the physically demanding labor of picking crops fell often on women and children. These contributions were sometimes overlooked in writing the history of the region. Neatly packaged histories often portrayed men as hard-working farmers, their wives as caretakers of the home, and children as attending one-room country schools. In reality, all members of the family worked hard, often out of doors, and picking crops could often supersede attending school.

Echoing Gilles' recollections, Emma Kleinknecht noted that her family grew "a lot of asparagus" on their twenty acres, "and us kids had to cut asparagus before the school bus came, or we didn't get to go to school."[23] Ilene Sparre similarly recalled that by age five "I had to pick a box of cherries in the morning and a box of cherries in the afternoon." Once, Sparre remembered, "I didn't get my box in the afternoon finished, so my dad and everybody sat down under the tree and wouldn't go home till I finished my box. Ever after that, I worked first, played later."[24] Kleinknecht also found herself in charge of milking the family cows, as the three daughters in the family were older than the three boys: "When I was eight years old, my dad came in the house, he says, 'Emma, you've got to learn to milk cows'.... And from then on, I milked cows."[25] Girls, as well as women, were often required to take on tasks that might have been considered masculine.

As with earlier generations of farm families, the dividing line between men's and women's work often blurred or disappeared entirely. While it was expected that women put in the hard work necessary to make homes from houses and keep the family fed, they were often also called upon to participate in the hard work of farming. Edith Hansen, whose father came to the area in 1915, recalled that during her childhood "when we hayed, we all hayed." While her father cut the hay and raked it into shocks to cure, Hansen and her siblings cleaned up any hay he missed. Then, once the crop was ready, Hansen's mother ran the horse team and derrick that lifted the hay to the top of the stack. Her father required further cooperation from her mother with other crops:

> [W]hen asparagus came into this country, why, then he plowed up a lot of his land and put it into asparagus. We had sixteen acres of asparagus. Now almost everybody in Richland had asparagus. But they had an acre or an acre and a half. And dad had sixteen acres. But anyway, he'd go down to Kennewick and get some fellows that didn't have work and bring them out. And mom would feed them. And they would work for him through the asparagus season.[26]

While Hansen did not elaborate on how many men worked for her father during these seasons, it would have been an immense amount of work to cook and clean dishes for these laborers during the harvest season. Hansen's mother's support in caring for the labor that harvested crops was a critical factor in the family's success.

Thanks to the efforts of women like Hansen's mother, who worked alongside their male counterparts, agricultural development continued steadily during the early twentieth century. By the time of World War I, White Bluffs' orchards were poised to reap the benefits of higher prices that crops brought in a better-connected market. Jeanie and Frank Wheeler, by this time decade-long residents and more experienced orchard growers, were able to expand their operations.[27] World War I necessitated nationwide rationing, but because so many residents already grew most of

Women and young girls participated in haying on farms in Richland and White Bluffs. *Harry Anderson Collection, East Benton County Historical Society.*

their own food, the Priest Rapids Valley communities were not impacted by wartime shortages nearly so much as other parts of the country. Following the war, an at-best marginally successful soldier settlement project brought new families to the area. Many of these arrivals struggled through hard times while waiting for just-planted fruit trees to mature. Wage work could be difficult to find at times. Even established residents like

Jeanie Wheeler were forced to seek additional employment—to supplement the family's income, she found work in a packing shed preparing produce for shipment to other markets.[28] The communities experienced hard times throughout the 1920s as a result of a drop in market prices following the war. This economic setback merged into the crisis of the Great Depression, and formed the backdrop of the decade during which many of the women interviewed as part of the Hanford History Project arrived. Despite the hard times, most recalled this time in the Priest Rapids Valley fondly.

Many of those who arrived during this time came as much in search of hope as relief. The combination of devastating decline of crop prices in the 1920s, the 1929 stock market crash, and the complete loss of crops as a result of the draught gripping the Midwest created a devastating set of conditions in which many families lost everything. Business owners and growers in the Priest Rapids Valley would suffer the effects of crop price decline as well. Jeanie and Frank Wheeler observed the irony of being advised "that there was not just overproduction, but extreme overproduction in a country where thousands, soon to be millions, were going hungry. The masses couldn't buy milk, let alone fruit." As a consequence, farmers across the country "were advised to start using as much of their own products as possible, rather than trying to sell on the crowded market."[29] This was nothing new for residents of White Bluffs, who had often done so when the costs of shipping fruit or low prices made selling produce less than economical.

In Jeanie's case, her years of wage work in White Bluffs packing sheds proved beneficial, and also signified women's political engagement. Having saved her pay stubs, she was able to apply for Social Security.[30] It was a triumph that validated Jeanie's decision to change her party affiliation from Socialist to Democrat in order to cast her vote for Franklin Delano Roosevelt in 1932.[31] In turn, some of Roosevelt's proposed plans to help the country directly impacted the Priest Rapids Valley. In addition to building projects including dams and roads, improved availability of electricity, and conservation programs, a new high school was erected at Hanford as part of a New Deal's Public Works Administration program. For many residents of the area, the Depression came to represent a time of coming together—community building during hard times. Because so many of the women interviewed for the Hanford History Project arrived during this time, and because the 1930s were the last decade that the Priest Rapids Valley communities would exist as residents knew them, this decade retains a near-mythic quality in their recollections.

Emma Kleinknecht insisted that her family suffered very little as a result of the Depression "because we raised everything we ate, my mom canned everything. And everything we had was from the ground. And none of us suffered from it. Because we had our own milk and those kinds of things." If White Bluffs suffered from economic downturn as a result of the Depression, it nonetheless maintained a good reputation for having productive land, and Kleinknecht, when asked if her family suffered any negative impacts from the Depression, somewhat romantically maintained that "Nope, them were the days."[32] It is surely a testament to how residents viewed the community that Kleinknecht continued to view it in such terms even many years after departing.

Ilene Sparre similarly recalled that if life was simple when her family arrived in Richland, none of her siblings seemed to mind. Her father "thought children was money because they could work on the farm, except, he had six girls, which kind of changed that," but the family weathered the Depression healthy and intact.[33] Other families were not so fortunate, and as the Midwest suffered through the effects of the Dust Bowl a new wave of hopeful settlers turned their sights west in search of relief. While perhaps not so famous as their counterparts who fled Oklahoma for the supposed Eden of California, many of the new arrivals made clear that they viewed the eastern Washington desert not just as a land of better opportunity than what they left behind, but as their only hope for survival.

Leatris Boehmer Reed was born in 1930, "a Depression baby," to parents already struggling to survive the effects of hard times in North Dakota. Around 1935, a younger brother died from the effects of what was likely asthma, an event that Reed believed "broke my mother's heart." In desperation, she "had written all over Washington [and] Oregon, because she knew that there was fruit there. And there was good [land], and the temperature was reasonable. And so, she wrote all the little towns that she could find in Washington and Oregon to find out what they did there, what they grew, and what the chances were of people surviving."

After sending dozens of letters, Reed's mother received replies from Mr. Reierson, the owner of White Bluff's grocery store, and from the owner of the White Bluffs bank. They wrote "glowing things about that there was work. There was packing sheds, there were alfalfa fields to take care of," and provided the family with hope.[34]

In contrast to the "Okies" immortalized by John Steinbeck's Joad family in *The Grapes of Wrath*, who arrived in California to discover no work and bitter disappointment, Reed's family found White Bluffs "exactly like they described it" upon arriving in 1936. "It was probably the best thing that ever happened to us, because we would have starved," Reed recalled during an emotional interview. They "had no money even to pay for that little boy's doctor bill that we left," but scraping together what little they owned, the rest of the family made it to White Bluffs. More than seventy years later Reed still recalled her first impressions of the place with a sense of awe and wonder, in marked contrast to what they left behind:

> We had electricity shortly before we moved from North Dakota because I remember my mother had a Maytag washing machine that she had just bought and paid $2 a month for. So, we had that all packed up and ready to go and our tickets—the government gave us tickets to get out of a depressed area. And we took the Empire Builder—brand new—to Spokane, and came into White Bluffs on a fruit train with our little parcel of stuff. And they welcomed us with open arms.

Reed remembered her mother's palpable relief at arriving in a community where if money was in short supply, a variety of produce and a strong sense of mutual support were present in abundance. Both were of equal importance.

"We had good neighbors, fruit orchards all over. All over. When they said that 'you will find all the fruit you want,' they really meant it," Reed explained. The family began growing alfalfa, because of the availability of good water on the farm where they settled, and because "alfalfa was a good-paying crop." But it was not the alfalfa, or even the family cow, that stood out in Reed's memory in describing her new surroundings. Recalling the presence of White Bluffs' abundant orchards, Reed noted that there was "every kind of fruit. First time I ever tasted cherries or even seen a cherry tree was there. Or ever ate an apricot or seen an apricot.

Or even apples—we had apples there—wonderful. And the whole valley was full of that. It wasn't just one little orchard, it was *lots* of orchards. It was covered with orchards and alfalfa fields."[35] For a family that arrived grieving the loss of a child and on the brink of starvation, White Bluffs was more than just an opportunity. It was a literal Eden of fruit orchards, where no one went hungry or without the support of neighbors.

In North Dakota, Reed recalled, even basic necessities like water had been hard to come by. Having "all the fresh water you needed" was viewed by Reed's mother as a blessing, "because we paid twenty-five cents a barrel in North Dakota for drinking water because it was rancid and acrid. Twenty-five cents then was a lot of money," and the family could ill-afford the expense. By the end of the family's first year in White Bluffs, Reed's mother could afford to give each child "two pennies for Jesus to take to Sunday school." Reed faithfully committed one penny each week to the church collection, but "I figured Jesus wouldn't care if I have a rope licorice from Pop English's [drugstore]." It was a luxury that would have seemed unthinkable in North Dakota a few months earlier. Reed's reminiscences are additionally significant in that they are representative of how many women remembered life in the community during the Depression.

Like Reed's parents, Ilene Sparre's father had looked to Washington to ensure a healthy life for his eight children. Though he had inherited eighty acres in Idaho from his own father, the Depression forced Sparre's father to acknowledge not only that "there wasn't any money in Idaho," but more importantly that "there wasn't a lot of food and it was very difficult. So, he managed to sell that and got this piece of property in Richland. And we built everything from scratch." Life still presented challenges, Sparre remembered, but,

> [W]e just loved it because we had not so much rain, like on the West Coast. And we had all that sagebrush to run around in. And it was just great living out there. And of course, we did what other farmers did. We saved food for winter. We canned, we froze. We had a dirt cellar. And my dad built our house. Wasn't too good at first, but it got better. Because there wasn't any money much, but we had a great life and lots to eat.[36]

Life may have been simple, but residents appreciated what the Priest Rapids Valley provided. Jean Johnson recalled that her family still relied on kerosene lighting, a wood stove, and an outhouse during much of the Depression. The family even made such necessities as toothpaste from "a little bit of soda and a little bit of salt," leading Johnson to consider her childhood as "very, very pioneer." Despite such circumstances, Johnson also insisted that family stories "made me think we were not poor."[37] For Johnson and others, not only plentiful food and water but a vibrant sense of community meant that material hardships were at worst nuisances, and at best built character. Catherine Finley summed up the sentiments of many former residents when, recalling her childhood, she insisted that "we didn't know we were supposed to be poor."[38]

Finley, like many others, felt that White Bluffs provided "all the good things in life," even if there was little to be had beyond necessities. Though times were admittedly hard, particularly during the 1930s, Finley describes feeling "very fortunate all during the Depression" that the family was "never hungry…I imagine the folks knew what the Depression was. Us kids didn't." Whereas Leatris Reed's family was unable to shield their children from the hardships of the Depression before relocating to White Bluffs, residents who lived there from the beginning were somewhat insulated from the worst of its effects. While manufactured goods were in short supply, Finley's family traded sheep with neighbors for fruit and other supplies and the family made most of the rest of what they needed. "We never had bought toys that I remember," Finley recalled. "My dad would carve things out of wood, out of mostly bark that come down the river…boats and mangers." The children often accompanied him to the river to collect driftwood and rocks, which "made wonderful trucks and cars and just any old thing…corrals to keep all these stick animals in."[39] There was a certain pride to be found in making do with what the area naturally offered. Residents like Finley maintained a sense of pride that they had experienced living in a way that embodied what their pioneer predecessors had withstood—while travel by train and automobile had made getting to the area easier, in many ways little had changed since true "pioneer days" or the hopeful advertisements of the first decade of the twentieth century.

In Finley's case, the sense of pioneer roots went much deeper than mere sentiment. Her father, Archie Borden, had been born in White Bluffs in 1898 and raised his family there. Finley's account of local businesses during her childhood included little beyond what had been advertised in 1908, yet the community did not consider itself to be lacking anything. Finley recalled that "on one side of the street there was a barber shop and drugstore and a grocery store.... And then there was a bank and a tavern and a little park where they had the bands and things and a post office and a tavern.... A couple of gas stations, the train depot and a creamery, or where everybody took their cream in for the Twin City Creamery to come out and get [it]." A hotel, promoted as the "$10,000 Hotel—the White Bluffs Inn, the noblest hotel in Central Washington" burned down in the 1930s after proudly serving the community for many years.[40] Jean Johnson, also born in White Bluffs to parents who had settled there as early as 1912, remembered that "we had stores. We had grocery stores. We had a barber shop. Had the power company. We had electricity at home," which enabled her mother to have both an electric and a wood stove.[41] It was more than many families had.

Finley, like others, recalled a close-knit, supportive community. "It was warm. It was a very warm community. The people were your friends. And they helped each other. If somebody needed something, somebody would either share or give or provide for them. And they didn't do it... just because family needed it at the time," Finley explained.[42] Lifetime residents of White Bluffs, like Finley, and transplants who arrived in the area much later similarly describe the sense of belonging that drew residents together, particularly women, who supported each other and children through difficult times. "I think it was a great life," Madeline Gilles echoed, "And of course there wasn't that many people, but they were good people."[43] For Leatris Reed, whose family arrived in desperate circumstances, the sense of community extended even to the children. In the tiny White Bluffs school, Reed recalled, "everybody helped everybody...it was probably the most together community" she had ever experienced.[44] Jean Johnson, born in White Bluffs in 1925, similarly recalled walking to school with three other girls, "carrying our lunch buckets and our books. And no fear. You know, every place we went, we walked. We had no fear. We knew everybody."[45]

The ability to give back became a particular source of pride for Reed's mother, who took special care to assist a reclusive artist who Reed recalls living in an abandoned building in a run-down section of the original

White Bluffs town site. He was "a real artist," as Reed recalled, and "my mother used to leave vegetables and fruit on his porch because she knew he didn't have a garden…. He was kind of a recluse," perhaps owing to rumors that he had once killed a man in self-defense. On Reed's tenth birthday, her mother took a second-hand bicycle to the artist, "and he painted roses on the fenders of that blue and white bike. And I had the prettiest bike in town," Reed fondly recalled. The bicycle, along with such memories, accompanied her out of White Bluffs when the family was forced to leave.[46]

If starvation was not a threat, the Depression brought other kinds of hardships. Many fell upon the area's oldest settlers. Jeanie Wheeler's widowed mother, Jane Shaw, for instance, found herself too poor to even afford "practical items such as yarn" for knitting, and the Wheelers found themselves unable to assist her. Though Jeanie and Frank assisted Jane in maintaining her orchard, "it was losing money like all of the others." Jane eventually began to receive public assistance checks for $25 a month, but "was soon cut off when a caseworker noted that she was receiving a magazine, *Comfort*, that cost a dollar a year. 'If you can afford this, you don't need welfare!' was the comment," and Jane never had her payments restored.[47]

While New Deal programs favored putting men to work, it often fell to women to maintain other aspects of family and community life. Murrel Dawson vividly recalled the pressure put upon her mother to keep the family functional while her father struggled with working the night shift at the Priest Rapids powerhouse, a job that kept him "working seven days a week with no days off" until eight o'clock each morning. "Mom would get up really early in the morning and take him down stuff so he could shave and get cleaned up and a change of clothes," Dawson recalled, "and she'd cook his breakfast. She always cooked his breakfast and took it down or whatever. Then she'd get us kids up, get us all fed, get us all cleaned up, dressed, in the car," either for school or, on special occasions, for shopping trips into Sunnyside or Hanford.[48]

While the orchards and gardens of White Bluffs provided abundant produce, preservation was another matter, as refrigeration remained a novelty even after electricity reached the town. Some families, like Dawson's, did not farm because of her father's work at the power plant. Dawson

Some women in Hanford and White Bluffs worked outside the home to help their families survive the Great Depression. These women worked at a fruit packing warehouse in Hanford. *Hanford History Project, Harry and Juanita Anderson Collection, RG4I_047.*

recalled groceries being delivered by Reierson's grocery store, and that "we never had fresh vegetables to speak of," because her mother immediately cooked and canned everything, including the meat.[49] Catherine Finley recalled in detail that canning food "was a whole family project" that required immense cooperation "because it all had to be done on a cook stove. And somebody had to bring in wood and peel fruit. It had to be continuous.… And that stove had to be kept burning. So, on that day also, if you were canning, you also made bread. Because the oven was hot."[50] Jean Johnson noted that as a child growing up in White Bluffs "we never had candy," but "we did have apple pie and chocolate cake" baked by their mother in abundance, "because we had so many apples, she was always making apple pie."[51] As in older times, the tasks of cooking and canning remained the purview of women.

When new technologies made their way into the Priest Rapids Valley, women sometimes had to master them on their own. Ilene Sparre recalled that starting the car was not only a responsibility her mother tackled head on, but a family effort:

One of my fondest memories as a child was trying to start the car. You had to crank it. And my mother was trying to start it but I was only three or four and I couldn't crank it fast enough. So, my other sister put her foot in on the clutch. And I put my foot on the gas. And we sit on the floor. And when mother said "let go of the clutch, and give it a little gas, but keep your foot on the brake," we did it. And we got it started. This, you know, three and four years old.[52]

In other cases, new technologies proved too much for men to handle and women found themselves in charge. Edith Hansen's mother found herself somewhat unexpectedly responsible for lighting the family home before electricity arrived in 1938. "Before that," Hansen remembered, "we had carbide," a type of lighting made by putting calcium carbide tablets into water. The family house was fitted with three carbide lights in the upstairs bedrooms, and one in the living and dining rooms. "My dad went down to Kennewick," Hansen recalled, "and the man said, now, don't let anybody touch this but you. You need to do this," implying that only a man should be in charge of such a thing. "And my mother run it all the time," Hansen laughed, "they didn't think a woman could handle the [carbide]. But they didn't know my dad. My dad was a farmer. He wasn't a gas man. Mom took over the gas." Hansen's family also briefly had a telephone—until her father "got so mad at the women visiting" on it that he tore it out.[53]

Hansen's recollections reveal other ways in which women were of central importance to the social life of their communities. When her parents bought an old house, "one of the first things they did was they built a great big concrete porch. And mom bought a piano for the girls to learn to play," and shortly thereafter the house became a gathering place for friends and neighbors as the family hosted dances. "The porch was wide enough and long enough you could get three square dances going," Hansen remembered, and there were "circles going on the porch. And the piano was in the living room. As we opened the door so they could hear the music."[54] Madeline Gilles similarly recalled that residents "used to have house parties in the wintertime. They'd clear the floor... and if there was a piano there, my mother played. And they danced or played cards."[55] Not all women enjoyed dancing. Emma Kleinknecht remembered that while her father enjoyed dances at the local Grange hall, and "danced with every lady," her mother stoutly refused. "So, I asked her why," Emma recalled. "She said, 'I'm a Sunday school girl.' But she never learned to dance."[56]

Many other families were active members of the local Grange, which in addition to dances held various activities such as fundraisers, lectures, and political discussions. Paula Bruggemann Holm's mother served as secretary of the Grange in 1939 and 1940. The Grange, notably, did not separate men's and women's activities, and "women in the Grange had

Women were active members of the local Grange organizations, as this 1917 photo of the Richland Grange taken in downtown Kennewick demonstrates. *Harry Anderson Collection, East Benton County Historical Society.*

equal status," rather than being "shunted off into separate auxiliaries."[57] There was also an active chapter of the Federated National Women's Club, to which Holm's mother belonged.[58] Founded in 1915 by Mrs. M. S. Meeks and federated the following year, the club quickly outgrew women's individual homes and eventually had to begin meeting in the Assembly Hall of the White Bluffs Lutheran Church. At least three women eventually attended the State Convention. "All of this developed a real friendship among us," one member later recalled, and it "educated us in various ways and broadened our outlook on life."[59]

Women engaged with the club in a variety of ways. Jeanie Wheeler served many turns as secretary-treasurer, and at least once, in 1926, as president. The club offered an impressive array of activities for local women, including "book reviews, musical performances, plays, even an art show," and also hosted discussions on a range of topics from "women's suffrage, Bible reading in the public school, modern Irish writers, and personal and property rights of women." Rather than a service-oriented organization, like the Grange, or the local Ladies Aid Society, the Women's Club was "a serious effort to imitate urban culture," and many White Bluffs women enjoyed the various activities it added to their lives.[60] Members also educated each other. "Some women came from most interesting backgrounds or had special interests and gave talks," it was later recalled, and "outside speakers" included "a lawyer and a business man" who discussed various issues.[61] The women who joined the White Bluffs Women's Club made very real contributions to the community,

The local Red Cross provided both opportunities for service and social gathering. This Red Cross Tea took place in April of 1918. *Hanford History Project, Harry and Juanita Anderson Collection, RG41_069.*

including purchasing trees and providing water to keep the local cemetery in good condition. "A men's group did the hard work," one woman later recalled, "but we helped, too, on 'cleanup day.'" These women were also responsible for establishing the first library in White Bluffs, which eventually became so popular that the state librarian "came over and organized it in a professional way."[62]

The strong sense of community, fostered by such organizations as the Grange, local churches, and clubs helped most Priest Rapids Valley residents weather the Depression fairly well. Despite the looming cloud of war, most signs pointed to better times on the horizon at the start of the 1940s. Crops had been "excellent" in 1942, markets were higher than they had been for more than a decade, and the community showed promising signs of good health.[63] No one could have predicted the unique devastation World War II would bring to White Bluffs and Hanford, or the instant transformation of Richland from a tiny farming community into a busy city.

As of December 6, 1941, life was still relatively normal. Jean Johnson recalled simply, "and then the war came." Johnson remembered that "the principal of the high school took us all in the next morning after Pearl Harbor," and informed the assembled students of the Japanese bombing of the American naval base.[64] Others heard the news huddled around tiny electric radios, or in the pages of the White Bluffs newspaper the following morning. "We knew about the war before then, except we weren't involved," Ilene Sparre recalled, "and then suddenly, we were involved. And then the government, Army, and everything—trucks—started rumbling into town."[65]

Aside from rationing that forced Sparre's mother to can fruit without sugar, women's greatest concern was for how the community suddenly changed. Before the war, Murrel Dawson recalled, "we never locked our houses out there. Nobody ever went into anybody else's house and took anything," and that extended to the local Wanapum Indians, who often stored things in several outbuildings near Dawson's home as they traveled between camps. As the area grew more crowded, "there were a lot of people that would come up, drive up, just sightseeing.… And the Indians didn't feel like their stuff was safe anymore," so they requested to store some items in the Dawson's basement. Her parents happily obliged, until the house was struck by lightning and burned to the ground. Dawson's parents moved up the valley to Priest Rapids, to a house "that the wind could blow dust through," and that loomed vividly in both her and her mother's memories:

> It was built in 1914 or something like that, and it was built flat on the ground. There was no foundation to lift it up. And it had guy-wires to keep it straight from the wind. It was guy-wired on the upwind side because the winds blew so hard that it…tilted, not a huge amount, but enough that they had to guy it up. And it was full of sand and dirt and leaves and whatnot, so Mom got in and cleaned it up…rolling news-papers up tight and lighting them on fire and making sure they weren't flaming but just cinders, and burning the black widows out from under the tub that sat on legs… And then once she got all that done, then us kids came up from Hanford and joined.[66]

Dawson's family spent several years living in the house while her father operated the Priest Rapids power plant. The family would live in several more houses before finally relocating to Yakima several years after World War II had ended.

Crop prices rose as the United States formally entered the war and the economy boomed for the first time in well over a decade, driven by wartime necessity. As late as 1943, most residents anticipated that per-haps the greatest challenge of the war years would be recruiting adequate labor to harvest crops with so many young men joining the armed forces. In this, too, women might likely have been called upon to fill a need, harvesting crops in wartime as they did in other parts of the country.[67] As with the possible economic revival of the communities, these matters "will always have a question mark attached," writ large by American ambi-tions to develop the first atomic weapons.[68] As with the men and women who arrived to work on producing the raw materials for the bombs, few residents could have foreseen how drastically and irreversibly life in the Priest Rapids Valley was about to change.

Leatris Reed's family lodged a husband and wife team of surveyors in their home in the months before the top-secret Hanford Site was officially declared. "They didn't even know what they were surveying for," Reed recalled, only that "they were hired by the United States government." The Reed children were fond of the couple, whom they affectionately called "Mama and Daddy Redd." Aside from enjoying their company and friendship, Reed recalled that Mrs. Redd "taught us really good things, things that we hadn't learned from our mom. Mama didn't know how to make fudge. She's never had that much sugar to spare in her life. So, we all learned how to make fudge and penuche and good stuff from Ma Redd."[69] Not long after the Redds departed, Reed's family, like others, was devastated by the sudden order to leave. Asked how she felt about moving to Walla Walla as a result of the removal orders, Reed spoke for many when she responded simply "Oh, I thought I was going to die!"[70] Allowed back many years later, Reed recalled that it "just broke my heart…there wasn't any stumps of trees left. There wasn't anything left."[71]

In the end, it was not the loss of land, crops, or houses that lingered most vividly in the minds of residents who were forced to relocate. The story of men being forced to leave behind homes, orchards ready to pick, and crops standing in the fields has long been recognized as one of the great tragedies of Priest Rapids Valley. Women's voices were not as often heard, but they suffered their own significant losses as a result of the order to leave. Asked what she wanted people to know about White Bluffs, Jean Johnson reiterated the thoughts of many pre-war residents in insisting simply that, "I want them to know that we had a community."[72]

For women, the sense of community displayed through gatherings such as those arranged by the Women's Club and the Grange were perhaps the most difficult to accept losing. Residents of the Priest Rapids Valley could build new homes, new farms, and new lives elsewhere, but the sense of belonging was something many profoundly missed and never recaptured. Even women who were relocated as children took note of the loss. "We had so much fun growing up in Richland," Ilene Sparre lamented, but Sunnyside, where the family relocated "was not that much fun." Sparre's mother resented the new "rules and regulations that we weren't accustomed to" living in the town, including a time when Sunnyside neighbors objected to her putting her daughters "in pants and shorts to play."[73] Murrel Dawson noted that while Priest Rapids was "an isolated area to live…it was a community, a close community."[74] Catherine Finley insisted that "it was a good place to live, good place to grow up in. And you learned a lot of things that you didn't know you learned."[75] Both women continued to mourn the loss of the community well into their adult lives. Years later, former residents began to organize an annual picnic, where they gathered to share memories of the communities they left behind. Jeanie Wheeler "in much later years enjoyed the accolades she got when she was the oldest person at the reunions," but never quite stopped mourning for what she'd left behind.[76] The picnics continued well into the following century, as Edith Hansen notes, though numbers have dwindled "down to about eight."[77]

For some women living in the Priest Rapids Valley, despite the hardships wrought by the Depression, there was still satisfaction to be found in simple things, like being able to provide meals, including apple pie for their families. This was a source of pride, and residents recognized that it was more than many had. For Leatris Reed, coming to the Priest Rapids Valley had meant the difference between starvation and survival. Understandably, leaving an area that had provided this sort of sustenance caused great anxiety. Further, Jean Johnson and others indicated there was much resentment caused by the reality that it was the families of service members who were forced to leave. These were not just women who made ends meet as farmers' wives—some, like Johnson's mother, had already made the sacrifice of sending sons off to war.

As women's memories of the Priest Rapids Valley prove, it was not an uninhabited desert when the government declared control over a 200,000-acre section in 1943. The communities of Hanford and White Bluffs had been growing along the banks of the Columbia River for decades. Both were forced to give way to the war effort. For families with deep roots in the area as well as more recent arrivals, many of whom were given less than two months to pack up their entire lives and vacate the only place that had ever felt like home, the experience of leaving proved far more painful than the ongoing hardships of the Great Depression had ever been. Looking back, Jean Johnson concluded, "it was a long trip from White Bluffs to Yakima in an old car."[78]

Notes

1. T. A. Larson, "Women's Role in the American West," *Montana: The Magazine of Western History*, 24: 3 (1974), 4.

2. By the later decades of the twentieth century, a new generation of historians had begun to produce "a small mountain of scholarship on women in the West, indicating deep and active fault lines in the terrain of western history as a whole." See Susan Lee Johnson, "'A Memory Sweet to Soldiers': The Significance of Gender in the History of the 'American West,'" *Western*

Historical Quarterly, 24: 4 (1993), 496. Among the earliest pieces to argue for the inclusion of women in the West was Joan M. Jensen and Darlis A. Miller, "The Gentle Tamers Revisited: New Approaches to the History of Women in the American West," *Pacific Historical Review*, 49: 2 (1980), 173–213. These historiographical interventions dramatically reshaped a century's worth of discussion about the West as an almost exclusively white male space. On multiculturalism in the West, see Elizabeth Jameson's "Toward a Multicultural History of Women in the Western United States," *Signs*, 13: 4 (1988), 761–91. Also crucial to revising scholarship on the West were Patricia Nelson Limerick's seminal work, *The Legacy of Conquest: The Unbroken Past of the American West* (New York: W. W. Norton, 1987); Susan Armitage and Elizabeth Jameson's edited volume, *The Women's West* (Norman: University of Oklahoma Press, 1988); and Sandra Myres' examination, *Westering Women: The Frontier Experience, 1800–1915* (Albuquerque: University of New Mexico Press, 1982).

3. On the role of Native female partners and Métis in the fur trade, see Sylvia Van Kirk, "From 'Marrying-In' to 'Marrying-Out': Changing Patterns of Aboriginal/non-Aboriginal Marriage in Colonial Canada," *Frontiers: A Journal of Women Studies* 7: 3 (2002), 1–11.

4. On Narcissa Whitman, see Julie Roy Jeffrey, "Narcissa Whitman: The Significance of a Missionary's Life," *Montana: The Magazine of Western History,* 41: 2 (1991), 2–15.

5. Martha Berry Parker, *Tales of Richland, White Bluffs & Hanford 1805–1943: Before the Atomic Reserve* (Fairfield: Ye Galleon Press, 1979); Otis W. Freeman, "Early Wagon Roads in the Inland Empire," *Pacific Northwest Quarterly*, 45: 4 (1954), 125–30.

6. Mary Powell Harris, *Goodbye, White Bluffs* (Yakima: Franklin Press, 1972), 34–35.

7. See, for instance, W.D. Lyman, *History of the Yakima Valley, Washington, Vol. I* (S.J. Clarke Publishing Company, 1919), available digitally at archive.org/details/historyofyakimav01lyma.

8. Harris, *Goodbye, White Bluffs,* 35.

9. Ibid., 36–37.

10. Murrel Dawson, interview by Robert Bauman, Hanford History Project (HHP), August 6, 2013.

11. Leatris Reed, interview by Robert Bauman, HHP, August 27, 2013.

12. Madeline Gilles, interview by Robert Bauman, HHP, July 2, 2013.

13. Nancy Mendenhall, *Orchards of Eden: White Bluffs on the Columbia, 1907 – 1943* (Seattle: Far Eastern Press, 2006), 19.

14. Ibid., 40–41.

15. Ibid., 32.

16. *Walla Walla* (WA) *Statesman*, March 20, 1908. The same advertisement appeared in newspapers from Seattle to Spokane, and in other states including Oregon, Idaho, and Montana.

17. Sherry L. Smith, "Single Women Homesteaders: The Perplexing Case of Elinore Pruitt Stewart," *Western Historical Quarterly*, 22: 2 (1991), 163.

18. Kathy Peiss, "'Vital Industry' and Women's Ventures: Conceptualizing Gender in Twentieth Century Business History," *The Business History Review*, 72: 2, Gender and Business (1998), 218–41.

19. Harris, *Goodbye, White Bluffs*, 39; see also science-ed.pnnl.gov/pals/resource/cards/ whitebluffs.stm.

20. Mendenhall, *Orchards of Eden*, 119.

21. Gilles interview.

22. Ibid.

23. Emma Kleinknecht, interview by Robert Bauman, HHP, June 12, 2013.

24. Ilene Gans Sparre, interview by Robert Bauman, HHP, August 28, 2013.

25. Kleinknecht interview.

26. Edith Hansen, interview by Robert Bauman, HHP, August 28, 2013.

27. Mendenhall, *Orchards of Eden*, 198.

28. Ibid., 326.

29. Ibid., 360.

30. Ibid., 385.

31. Ibid., 380.

32. Kleinknecht interview.

33. Sparre interview.

34. Reed interview.

35. Ibid.

36. Sparre interview.

37. Jean Johnson, interview by Robert Bauman, HHP, July 31, 2013.

38. Catherine Borden Finley, interview by Robert Bauman, HHP, July 9, 2013.

39. Ibid.

40. Catherine Finley interview; *Walla Walla Statesman*, March 20, 1908.

41. Jean Johnson interview.

42. Finley interview.

43. Gilles interview.

44. Reed interview.

45. Johnson interview.

46. Reed interview.

47. Mendenhall, *Orchards of Eden*, 384.

48. Dawson interview.

49. Ibid.

50. Finley interview.

51. Johnson interview.

52. Sparre interview.

53. Hansen interview.

54. Ibid.

55. Gilles interview.

56. Kleinknecht interview.

57. Mendenhall, *Orchards of Eden*, 180.

58. Paula Bruggemann Holm, interview by Robert Bauman, HHP, August 6, 2014.

59. Letter Describing the White Bluffs Women's Club, Harry and Juanita Anderson Collection, HHP.

60. Mendenhall, *Orchards of Eden*, 177.

61. Letter Describing White Bluffs Women's Club.

62. Ibid.

63. Mendenhall, *Orchards of Eden*, 402.

64. Johnson interview.

65. Sparre interview.

66. Dawson interview.

67. For more on this aspect of women's service in World War II, see Stephanie Ann Carpenter, "'Regular Farm Girl': The Women's Land Army in World War II," *Agricultural History,* 71: 2 (1997), 162–85.

68. Mendenall, *Orchards of Eden*, 25.

69. Reed interview.

70. Ibid.

71. Ibid.

72. Johnson interview.

73. Sparre interview.

74. Dawson interview.

75. Finley interview.

76. Mendenhall, *Orchards of Eden*, 418.

77. Hansen interview.

78. Johnson interview.

CHAPTER FOUR

"It Was Like an Invasion!"

The Federal Government and the Displacement of Peoples in the Priest Rapids Valley

Robert Bauman

Driving northwest on State Highway 240 out of Richland, you begin to see the Hanford Nuclear Reservation to your right. Driving past the vast expanse that is Hanford takes what seems like an eternity. Off in the distance you can see some of the handful of buildings from the World War II and Cold War years—mostly cocooned reactors in the 100 Area and buildings in the 200 Area where the nuclear waste is stored in tanks, some of which have leaked or are leaking into the desert soil. After about thirty miles, Highway 240 ends, becomes Highway 24, and veers north. A few miles down Highway 24, as you reach the far northwest corner of the Hanford Site, a structure can be seen in the distance. From the road, it is difficult to determine exactly the nature of the building, but it is clearly not an industrial building related to nuclear processing. Instead, this is a building related to the settlement of people.

Visible from Highway 24 is, indeed, one of the few remnants of the rural settlements and towns that appeared in the late nineteenth and early twentieth centuries along the Columbia River in the Priest Rapids Valley, only to largely disappear when the federal government ordered the evacuation of the area to make way for a wartime project. The building is known as the Bruggemann cookhouse, named for the Bruggemann family who lived on the property and farmed the surrounding land until March of 1943. Paul Bruggemann, a German immigrant, his wife Mary,

91

and their two children, Ludwig and Paula, were living in their home a stone's throw from the Columbia River in March 1943 when they received notice that they had to leave. Uprooted from their home, the Bruggemann family eventually resettled in Yakima. The cookhouse on their former property stands as a lonely reminder of their previous lives and of the rural communities long since gone.[1]

The Bruggemann family cookhouse is located at the far northwest corner of the Hanford Nuclear Reservation. Constructed from river rock in the early twentieth century, this building is one of the few extant reminders of the small farming communities evacuated by the federal government in 1943 to make way for Hanford. *Robert Bauman, 2012.*

On March 6, 1943, just days after Japanese Americans throughout the West Coast of the United States were notified they were going to be forcibly removed to internment camps, all of the residents, including the Bruggemanns, of the small towns of Hanford and White Bluffs, and some in Richland, received letters from the federal government notifying them that they had approximately thirty days to leave their land to make way for a secret government war project. The notice informed residents that the government would appraise the land and purchase it for the price their appraisers determined. The people of the area would have no choice in the matter. This chapter uses the voices of the former residents of the towns of Hanford, White Bluffs, and Richland to tell their stories of evacuation from their homes and to uncover some of the spaces of meaning of towns, farms, and communities that no longer exist.

Of course, the removal of people from their land by the federal government was nothing new in 1943, particularly for Native peoples. Indeed, federal Indian removal policy began with Andrew Jackson and the forced removal of the Five Civilized Tribes from Georgia that led to the Trail of Tears in the 1830s. While the federal government forcibly moved some Native peoples ever further west, those Native groups who lived in the trans-Mississippi West eventually faced relocation as well. However, instead of moving these groups further west, the government, beginning in the 1850s, forced Natives in the West, like the Yakama, the Umatilla, and the Nez Perce, onto reservations. So, when the federal government notified the residents of White Bluffs, Hanford, and Richland that they would need to evacuate their land, what was new was not the process of removal, but who was being removed. This time, in addition to removing some Native peoples like the Wanapum tribe off their land, the federal government was removing white settlers as well.[2]

Responses to the evacuation notices received in March 1943 in the towns of White Bluffs, Hanford, and Richland, ranged from resignation to shock and disbelief, to anger and bitterness. Annette Heriford grew up in Hanford and later became one of the leaders of the White Bluffs-Hanford Pioneer Association, which for decades held annual picnics, bringing together former residents to reminisce about their towns, farms, and previous lives. Decades after the forced evacuation of their homes, Heriford remained nostalgic about those former lives and bitter about what happened to her family, their land, and her town. In 1984, she recalled: "In March 1943, when I was about 22, we received a letter from the government saying that we would have to move in 30 days. It was a terrible shock. I can't describe it. It was unbelievable.... It was a terrible blow."[3] Heriford also recalled that "the last thing we were thinking was that somebody was going to say, 'you have to be out in 30 days.'"[4]

Jerome Clarke, another Hanford resident, remembered that he and his wife Alene were doing better by 1943 as wartime prices helped them make ends meet and see a slight profit. As Clarke remembered, "our soft fruit was giving us income enough to put in pressure water, sink and cabinets and other necessities." But that all changed when the Clarkes received their letter from the government on March 6, 1943. According to Clarke, their "fruit trees were well on the way for a good crop in June 1943 when [the government] informed us…that from that day on all crops were the property of the U.S. government." The Clarkes, and some other farmers in the area who found themselves in similar circumstances, signed a contract to farm their crops for DuPont. Clarke noted that most

An aerial view of the town of Richland before the Army issued evacuation orders to its residents and the residents of White Bluffs and Hanford. Within several months, the farms in this photo were bulldozed to make way for the Hanford Engineer Works. *Harry Anderson Collection, East Benton County Historical Society.*

important to them "was the fact that by working for DuPont, [we] were able to stay in our homes…for one year, which gave us time to find a place to relocate."[5]

Indeed, those in the area who had survived the Great Depression in 1942 felt hope for the first time in years as prices for their crops rose to the point that they could make a bit of a profit. As former White Bluffs resident Walt Grisham remembered: "we had gone through the depression by the skin of our teeth, things began to look up a little bit, the farm situation began to look like our products would get some profit. At the very time that things began to look good—the bottom got pulled out from under you. The government came…. We had apricot trees out with the first real crop on it and they would not let us pick it." Instead, families like the Grishams were forced to leave their land, and prisoners from Columbia Camp located at nearby Horn Rapids were brought in to pick the apricots and other fruit. Local families had to leave before they could harvest their own fruit. Years later Grisham said he was not bitter about what had happened, but "disappointed in the way that it was done…. Those people could have gone ahead and harvested their fruit, got their money, packed and moved on. But no, they wouldn't let them do it."[6]

While most of the residents of the town of Richland were not evacuated, those who lived on farms on the outskirts were forced to leave their homes. But, because their farms were not located on the central part of the Hanford Site, many Richland residents who were given evacuation notices were allowed to stay longer than most residents in Hanford or White Bluffs. Gordon Kaas grew up on a forty-acre farm a few miles north of the town of Richland. He remembers as an eleven-year-old boy seeing a number of cars driving around the area in February and March of 1943. Then his parents told him "that the whole community, including White Bluffs and Hanford, was being evicted for a government project." Because the Kaas family farm was located in north Richland it was outside of the central Hanford Engineer Works area. As a result, the Kaas family was allowed to stay for the entire growing season and did not have to move out until November 1943. Even so, the family felt pressure to move as their house was being held to give to a Hanford patrol officer, and as Kaas remembers, the patrol officer "was anxious to move in." Eventually, the Kaas home became the office for the trailer camp that housed thousands of Hanford workers. Indeed, the house was used by various Hanford contractors until it was torn down in the 1990s, one of the last remaining remnants of pre-1943 farm life in Richland.[7]

Richland resident Robert Fletcher was enrolled in the Reserve Officer Training Corps (ROTC) as a junior at Washington State College in Pullman in January 1943, when he was drafted by the Army. He traveled back to Richland to see his family and sweetheart, Betty Kinsey, briefly before heading to Fort Lewis for basic training. About a month later his parents told him that they had been informed that the entire Priest Rapids Valley would "be taken over by the government for this Hanford project." While most residents of the valley had only thirty days to vacate their land and homes, the Fletcher family was able to stay longer because Fletcher's father, Francis, was the manager of the irrigation district in Richland and the Army Corps of Engineers believed it would be helpful to keep him at his job.[8]

Ray Deranleau, who also lived in Richland, tells the following story about his family receiving word that they were going to be moved off of their property. "We got notice from the government on March 6…a little bit before noon, in the mail. And I was plowing a field and I came in for lunch, and they [his parents] were telling me about it. And after I ate, I went back out and cranked up that tractor. And I bet I hadn't been plowing an hour and a half and somebody called up there and told them to get that tractor out of that field."[9]

Residents of White Bluffs had reactions to the evacuation order similar to the residents of Hanford and Richland. Frank and Jeanie Wheeler had arrived in White Bluffs in 1907 and had worked hard for over thirty years to establish their forty-acre homestead. Now they were being told they would have to evacuate in thirty days. According to author Nancy Mendenhall, "the Wheelers stared at their orders in disbelief. They and their neighbors had…to give up their homes, businesses, orchards and fields, and move out." When they were told it was for a top-secret government wartime project, they "could not dream what the project was. Since it was top secret, Frank deduced it was to produce a deadly weapon, some kind of poison gas. But why couldn't it be a temporary move until the war was over…and why did the project have to be in their perfect farming area?"[10] Priest Rapids Valley residents were left wondering why they were being forced to permanently leave the land they had farmed for decades.

Lloyd Wiehl, whose parents operated the White Bluffs ferry and had lived in White Bluffs from the early days of the town's existence, remembered that the news of the forced evacuation "came like a bombshell. They announced they were taking the whole valley. For what? We didn't know. At that time, the farmers were short of money and didn't have any place to go."[11] Other families had similar experiences.

Kathleen Hitchcock grew up in White Bluffs, the daughter of Tom and Jane O'Larey, who owned and printed the local newspaper, the *White Bluffs Spokesman*. Her parents had moved to White Bluffs in 1910 and, in addition to publishing the newspaper, owned a ten-acre apple farm. Hitchcock recalled that the evacuation "was a pretty hard thing.... My mother never really adjusted to it...the fact that the government could come in and take your home away. We were in the war and they felt like they were donating as many young men as any other place to the war effort. It was really sad.... They resented the whole thing, even knowing it was for the war effort. They felt it was too great a sacrifice."[12]

In a letter she penned to Alene Clarke of the White Bluffs-Hanford Pioneer Association, former White Bluffs resident Sally Brown Gonzales expressed her regrets at her inability to attend the annual pioneers' picnic in 2000. Her father, Jess Brown, had owned a barbershop in White Bluffs and her mother, Julia Marsh Brown, taught at the White Bluffs School. In her letter, Gonzales reflected on the permanent impact of the 1943 evacuation on her family: "I was only 5 years old when we were evacuated and my father and mother had to leave his business, our home, everything and just walk out and shut the door. It's made a lasting impression on me that's not easy to put into words."[13]

Catherine Finley, who grew up in White Bluffs and was in sixth grade in the spring of 1943, recalled how the evacuation impacted her parents' generation: "It was hard for my dad because he had lived there his whole life.... The fruit farmers had to leave their crops on their trees. And that was very hard on them, no future, no money, cash in hand...they moved wherever they could get a place to live.... My dad sold sheep and sold most of the cattle, kept a couple of the horses."[14]

According to Finley, her family was "the very last ones out there." Her father, Archie, was a refrigeration engineer who made ice for the railroad that had a station in Hanford. DuPont and the Army Corps of Engineers continued to use the railroad and needed ice for the food for the thousands of new workers arriving to build and operate Hanford. So Archie Borden kept his job and his family stayed on their land in White Bluffs for at least eighteen months after first receiving their notification of evacuation. Some of the DuPont employees moved into some of the recently vacated homes. According to Finley, DuPont would "put two families to a home if there was enough for two bedrooms, because there was no housing for all of these thousands of people coming in.... Any house that had been vacated, that's how they utilized them.... It was DuPont that come and took our house. We weren't happy about that."[15]

In addition to his home and land in White Bluffs, Archie Borden owned an island located in the Columbia River just across from the town of White Bluffs. Finley remembered her father being "very proud of that island because there was a large Indian cemetery on it. And he guarded that with his life to keep it from being dug. And several times during the night, he'd go. If he saw a bonfire over there, he'd go down to the river and go across it and get the people off the island...he guarded that cemetery with his eye teeth." But, as part of the preparation for the Hanford Site, Borden sold the island to the federal government, which eventually turned it over to the state Department of Fish and Wildlife.[16]

Children in families like the Bordens and Kaases, able to stay in the area longer than thirty days, continued school in the spring of 1943, but the children attended school six days a week, instead of five. This enabled the students to complete their school year early, so their families could then be evacuated from the site. Indeed, the final day of classes for students in Hanford and White Bluffs who attended a combined school in Hanford that included the children of some DuPont employees living temporarily in some of the homes in Hanford, was May 15, 1943, about two to three weeks earlier than usual.[17]

Jack Collins and his family moved to White Bluffs during the Great Depression and bought a ten-acre farm. Several years later, Jack's father was hired to be the head operator at the Priest Rapids power plant and the Collins family purchased a thirty-five-acre farm near the plant, in addition to the farm they already owned. According to Collins, when the federal government evacuated most of the population, "they kept my dad on…to pump water for all the construction in the water districts.… Dad pumped the water for the construction of the railroads and the roads.… When the government finished construction and they were ready to start operating the plants, they had us move out.… We lost our farms.… My folks had very little money when they left there." For Collins and his family, the timing of the forced evacuation was especially gut-wrenching. According to Collins, "we were going to plant 15 or 16 acres of apricots on our place. We lost all our deposit and everything. The government could've cared less."[18]

Collins also remembered that the forced evacuation was especially difficult for certain groups of individuals. He noted that, "it wasn't good for…the older people, the widows and widowers.… They ended up in institutions. They had no family. They had no one. And the government just forced them out."[19]

Mendenhall agreed. She noted that "the older people didn't have the strength to start new farms, and their compensation was not enough to buy into working farms. In the end, most of them settled in small homes in the farming towns of eastern Washington. With their friends and neighbors scattered to the winds, social supports along with them, they would have a lot of time on their hands and meager livings." And, like all of the residents of the towns in the Priest Rapids Valley, they were losing the spaces and places of meaning to them.[20]

Much of the bitterness that remained long after 1943 for former Hanford, White Bluffs, and Richland residents was related to what they saw as low appraisals and prices for their family homes and farms. Government appraisers were instructed to produce appraisals for over 2,000 tracts of land in the Priest Rapids Valley in a short period of time. Some residents accepted the government's offer because they felt they had no choice and that it was the patriotic thing to do. Indeed, by June 1943 the federal government had failed to pay those residents who had agreed to the government's price. As a result many of those residents, who had little money, refused to leave until they received their payment for their land. Some remained throughout the summer of 1943.[21]

Jay Perry, an independent appraiser hired by the town residents, remembered that when residents received their notifications in March 1943, "if a bomb had been dropped in the community it would not have caused any more uproar. I liken it to what happens when one kicks a hive of bees." Perry remembered:

> [G]radually it became known that the Government planned to acquire 400,000–500,000 acres in northern Benton County and across the Columbia River in Franklin County on which some kind of plant connected with the war effort would be built.... [Residents] would have to move in 30 days. When it became apparent that everyone could not be moved out within 30 days a change was made and only those whose lands were needed at once were required to move within that time, extending some zones to fall of that year.... A provision in the condemnation proceedings allowed an owner who was not satisfied with the offer by the condemning body to go into court and accept 90 percent of the offer without prejudice to his later claim for more money. This, many landowners did to get themselves money with which to move.[22]

Some residents appealed to those in power. Jeanie Wheeler wrote a letter complaining about the low appraisals to Senator Homer Truett Bone, who served as senator from Washington State from 1933 to 1944. Bone was a Democrat and an isolationist who had opposed American entry into World War II until Pearl Harbor. Bone's response to Wheeler highlighted the secrecy surrounding Hanford: "So far none of us have been able to learn the exact purpose of the acquisition, the Department shrouding it in mystery." His response also suggested that he supported the residents' cause. Bone told Wheeler, "I can assure you, my protest to the Department over this matter was vigorous. I wish I had the authority to compel the appraisal of lands at a value reflecting what my correspondence seems to indicate to be the real value."[23]

Some residents accepted the government's first, second, or third offers, but by April 1944, over a year after residents first received notice that they were going to need to evacuate the area, the War Department had been able to reach agreements with landowners on only 683 tracts of land, leaving almost 1,400 unsettled. Those cases were forwarded to the Justice Department for settlement or trial. The War Department admitted that this was "an extraordinarily high proportion of tracts left for disposition in court," noting that normally in cases where they had purchased homes and land, 90 percent of tracts purchased were settled amicably.[24]

The War Department acknowledged several reasons for the high percentage of unsettled cases. First, it highlighted confusion over the varying dates when it took possession of individual properties. In an effort to accommodate property owners and for "the very laudable purpose of saving all the food which could be saved for the war effort," the War Department permitted land owners in areas which were not needed for immediate construction to remain in possession of their properties in order to harvest crops. Some land owners, like the Kaas family, were able to harvest all of their crops, others a portion of their crops, and some not at all. This greatly affected appraisals. A combination of bumper crops and steadily increasing prices during the war "widened the differences of opinion between the War Department and the owners as to value."[25]

In addition, the speed with which the appraisers had to work undoubtedly impacted their appraisals. Given the time constraints, appraisers inevitably rushed some of their work. And some appraisers used their own methods rather than the ordinary market value established by the government for their appraisals. This created uneven and inequitable appraisals. Indeed, the inequity of the government appraisals can be seen in the fact that by May 1944, seventy-seven cases had already gone to trial and in all of them the money given to the landowners "greatly exceeded" the values fixed by the War Department appraisers.[26]

In an effort to make some of these cases more equitable, the War Department did pay some landowners for the net value of their crops. For instance, Ben and Elise Moede were paid an additional $2,000 for their crop of apricots and peaches. The War Department estimated the total value of the Moedes' crops at $2,081, but deducted $81 for the labor provided by the nearby prison camp to pick the fruit. Apparently, that was not enough to satisfy Mr. Moede, as he refused to settle and was one of the residents who pursued his case against the federal government in court.[27]

Some citizens in the town of Richland decided to hire independent appraisers to conduct their own estimates of their property values. Many residents felt the appraisals from the War Department were too low to compensate for not only the loss of their homes and land, but also the cost of moving and buying homes elsewhere at a time when land prices were rising rapidly. Officers of the Richland Irrigation District encouraged Priest Rapids Valley residents to refuse to sign the offers presented by the War Department due to what they considered the low levels of the appraisals. The Irrigation District hired a group of independent appraisers, including Jay Perry, to set values on all property in the district to demonstrate the undervaluation of property in the Priest Rapids Valley by the appraisers working for the Army Corps of Engineers. The Irrigation District officers, including Francis Fletcher, father of Robert Fletcher, argued that since it was "a military necessity for them to move, our farmers should be re-established elsewhere in somewhat comparable circumstances to that out of which they have been moved by government order. It is unfair…to put a cold-blooded commercial appraisal on our homes."[28]

Indeed, according to Robert Fletcher, his father Francis became "one of the leaders" of the group of valley residents that pursued a better offer for their land and ended up taking the federal government to court. As Fletcher explained in an oral history interview in 2013, "my folks and others were beginning to feel established, that here they'd worked most of their working lives for 12, 15 years getting to where they felt like they…

The Fletcher family home is one of the few original homes from the town of Richland that still exists today. The home was used by government officials for several years and is now owned by a private party. *Robert Bauman, February 2017.*

could make a good living. And now they were being offered this, where they had to leave relatively quickly. And not being offered enough to buy something comparable in other areas, where they found they had to pay more than what they had been offered." The court case took years before it was settled and Fletcher's parents "were not too happy about" the final settlement.[29]

The Kaas family had a similar appraisal experience. Gordon Kaas remembered, "those people that were here driving in cars were appraisers. And they were going around and appraising the farms.... Some [residents] got very nervous. They thought if you didn't take the first offer, they might just haul you out in handcuffs.... My father accepted the third appraisal and got $7,200."[30]

The records provide numerous examples of Richland residents who had received low offers from the government. For instance, H. H. Mowry's five acres of cultivated land was valued by government appraisers at $600, even though in 1942 Mowry had grossed $1,200 from the crops alone. A year earlier, Albert Hackney had been offered $2,500 for his land. The government appraised it at $1,700. And Bernie Fruehling had purchased five acres of grapes, prunes, and peaches in 1941 for $2,000. In 1943, the government appraised his property for $1,750. The Irrigation District officials then summed up their argument: "The distressing point is that scores of families are now living in reasonable comfort and security in their elderly age, largely free of mortgage worries, and that it is entirely impossible for them to re-locate themselves elsewhere with what the government has allowed them."[31]

Other former residents of the region interviewed as part of the Hanford Oral History Project told similar stories. Lloyd Chalcraft was in eighth grade in March 1943 when his family received notice of their impending removal from their land in Richland. Chalcraft remembered: "People were mad because they [the government] come in here and took this land over. They practically stole the land. I mean, people were really shook up.... They didn't know what was going on. It was like an invasion."[32]

Chalcraft's parents received $700 for their ten-acre plot of farmland. His grandfather, Thomas, received $1,300 for his twenty-five-acre cherry orchard. Chalcraft's family moved quickly, within the thirty-day time frame given by the government, to a new home in Kennewick. In part, they moved quickly to assure themselves a good place to move to once they had to leave Richland.[33]

Former White Bluffs resident Bernard Worby had a similar response when asked about the appraisal of his family's land in his oral history interview conducted decades later. According to Worby, his family received $500 for a ten-acre irrigated fruit farm. Worby's resentment remained fifty years later: "The government stole our property. I still resent that it happened."[34]

Annette Heriford also remembered the low initial appraisal her family received from government appraisers. According to Heriford, the government appraisers initially valued her family's thirty acres at $1,700. Heriford's father was one of the many residents to sue the government and win. Following the lawsuit, the Heriford family received $3,200 for their thirty acres, almost doubling the government's initial offer.[35]

Frank and Jeanie Wheeler's experience was similar to the Heriford family. Their initial appraisal valued their forty acres, with three houses, twenty acres of orchards, and an irrigation system, at a meager $1,500. Following their lawsuit handled by attorneys Lloyd Wiehl and Charles Powell, the Wheelers eventually received $6,500 for their land. After being removed from their property, the Wheelers initially moved to Seattle to stay with their daughter, Margaret, and once they received their settlement after the war, they moved into a small home on Bainbridge Island.[36]

The Clarke family also benefitted from not accepting the government's offers. Government appraisers valued the Clarkes' property at $6,500. But the Clarkes hired Wiehl and took their case to court. It was a smart move. The court decided in the Clarkes' favor and valued their land at $30,500. The Clarkes used the money from the court decision to buy a new place in nearby Kennewick.[37]

Indeed, the controversy over appropriate compensation for the former residents of the towns in the Priest Rapids Valley attracted regional interest. In December 1944, the *Seattle Times* published a three-part investigative series on the issue. Earlier that month, some former residents had called for a congressional investigation arguing that representatives of the War Department had pressured residents to take low appraisals and had provided erroneous information to residents. R. S. Reierson, the former owner of the drugstore in White Bluffs, who also served as secretary of the Priest Rapids Irrigation District and evacuation chair of the Benton County Civilian Defense Council, told the *Seattle Times* reporter that government agents questioned his patriotism when he refused their initial offer. According to Reierson, he had been offered $1,800 for a farm that cost him $3,000. He told the negotiator he had been willing to sacrifice his property if it was of importance to the government, "but when he came around in the manner in which he did, [Reierson] was insulted." Reierson and his five brothers had served in World War I and he was offended that anyone would question his patriotism, telling the reporter, "he couldn't tell me what patriotism is. I know what it is to serve my country."[38]

Indeed, patriotism played a role in the decisions of other residents of White Bluffs against challenging government appraisals of their property values. Dale McGee and Yvonne Ponsat McGee, both former residents of White Bluffs, remembered that their fathers, both veterans of World War I, refused to challenge government appraisals out of a sense of patriotism. According to Yvonne McGee, her and Dale's fathers "would not fight the government over the compensation for their ranches…. They were not interested in litigation. They did not want to fight the government because they felt like if the government needed it, they should let them have it."[39]

Lloyd Wiehl, the attorney from Yakima who along with Charles Powell represented many of the former residents, led the request for a congressional investigation. Wiehl, who grew up in White Bluffs, recounted the stories of several former residents whose offer from the federal government was much lower than the appraisal value given by independent appraisers. For example, Evelena Boie, a widow from Hanford, was offered $3,250 by government officials, but independent appraisers valued her property at $6,000. George Sommers was offered $2,300 for his home and nine acres of land; independent appraisers valued his land at $10,000. The War Department initially offered Thomas Sigurdson $12,500 for his home and fruit orchard. Sigurdson refused to accept the offer and when his property was re-evaluated by appraisers from the Department of Justice who were assigned to the unsettled cases, he received a new offer of $19,000.[40]

Sigurdson believed the difference in appraisal values could be explained in part by the fact that the initial appraisers working for the War Department were from the Federal Land Bank in Spokane. Those men had spent their careers trained to value property at the lowest possible value in order to get profit from their mortgages. In addition, the War Department appraisers were appraising for loan value rather than market value, a significant difference.[41]

While many former residents of Hanford and White Bluffs remained bitter decades later, others had come to an acceptance of what had happened. Dick Wiehl, whose grandparents operated the White Bluffs ferry and whose attorney father Lloyd represented the residents—including his own parents—who sued the government over their land appraisals, was a young boy of seven when his grandparents received the news that they would need to leave. As Wiehl remembered, at the time, "all heck broke loose…we've got to get out. Where are we going to go?" As Wiehl described, since his grandparents "had their own house attorney" they sued the government and "in 1946 or 1947 they received fair value for the acreage that the government had taken." With the money his grandparents received, they were able to purchase what Wiehl described as "a huge ranch" near Cle Elum. No doubt because they eventually received a fair price for their land and were able to purchase a large ranch with the money from the government, Wiehl's grandparents "never argued or never felt badly about contributing to the quicker end of the war by the building of the atomic bomb. They felt pretty good about it, I think, that they had made a contribution." Clearly, those families who eventually received what they believed was a reasonable compensation for their land and had enough resources to emerge from this period in solid financial standing held less bitterness toward the government about their removal.[42]

Some residents did not remain bitter toward the government at all. Former White Bluffs resident Claude Rawlins remembered his family was angry about the low appraisal for their farm, but they moved "because the law required it and…there was a war on…. We didn't hate the government over it, we hated DuPont [the DuPont Corporation was the first contractor hired to operate the Hanford Site]. I remember never buying a DuPont product after that…if it said DuPont, we didn't buy it. There was the Japanese and the Germans and DuPont—those were the enemies."[43]

For some residents of the Priest Rapids Valley, leaving their land was part of their patriotic duty. They were not happy about it, but they felt they had no choice and were sacrificing for the good of the country.

The last residents of Hanford and White Bluffs to be moved to make way for the Hanford Site were those no longer living. As Lloyd Chalcraft remembered, "The government dug all those [graves] up.... How could they let people go there if there's top secret stuff? How could they let people go out there and wander around the cemetery? There'd be all kinds of people wandering around, wouldn't there? The government removed all of them bodies. Some of the families got the bodies. But most of the bodies were moved to Prosser."[44]

Shortly after the Army Corps of Engineers began construction of the Hanford Engineer Works, project personnel ascertained the existence of three cemeteries and several burial grounds within the boundaries of the site. Project engineers decided that White Bluffs Cemetery along with burial grounds located on the land of the Boie, Anglin, and Wiehl families, all needed to be moved. In addition, project staff estimated that approximately 1,500 Indian graves existed in the area, but the graves were unmarked and their exact locations unknown. Native peoples would not have the option of having their graves moved.[45]

In May 1944, Hamilton Mortuary of Vancouver began moving graves from the White Bluffs Cemetery (which housed the dead of both the towns of Hanford and White Bluffs) to the cemetery in Prosser, a small town about twenty miles southwest of the Hanford Site. Edmund Anderson, a former White Bluffs resident, had spent over a year in some cases trying to contact relatives to receive permission to remove their loved ones' remains to Prosser. Anderson was president of the White Bluffs Cemetery Association, which met in May 1943 to determine the disposition of the graves at the White Bluffs Cemetery. It was at that meeting that the association decided to have the federal government move the bodies to the new cemetery in Prosser. If residents wanted their relatives' remains removed to somewhere other than Prosser, they had to make separate arrangements and pay for the costs themselves. While the vast majority of the 177 remains were removed from the White Bluffs cemetery, several had to be disinterred from gravesites on former family farms where the relatives had been buried. Anderson, who had a wife, mother, and daughter buried in the White Bluffs Cemetery, was present every day to ensure the proper removal and reburial of the graves. Anderson also arranged for the War Department to hold a dedication ceremony at the Prosser Cemetery in 1944. A number of former White Bluffs and Hanford residents attended the ceremony to honor their family members.[46]

The monument erected by Edmund Anderson and the White Bluffs Grange to honor the deceased from Hanford and White Bluffs whose remains were moved to the Prosser Cemetery in 1944. *Robert Bauman, January 2017.*

Following the cemetery dedication ceremony, Anderson penned a letter to the residents of Prosser thanking them for their kindness "in permitting us to move our departed relatives to your beautiful cemetery." Anderson noted that he had investigated other places, "but no one else welcomed us and some even refused to consider the matter." According to Anderson, though, "Prosser's attitude was different." Anderson noted "there was no hesitation" on the part of the cemetery association there to accept the former residents of White Bluffs and Hanford. Anderson closed his letter saying that he considered the Prosser Cemetery "the most beautiful cemetery in any small city in the state." He also concluded that he was pleased "that this unpleasant business should be terminated so satisfactorily." Residents of Hanford and White Bluffs had lost their spaces and places of memory—

their farms, homes, churches, schools. Carving out a new space in the Prosser Cemetery for their departed loved ones helped provide a place of meaning and memory for some former residents.[47]

To some former residents of Priest Rapids Valley, though, the removal of their relatives' graves was one final blow to a place that had held so much meaning for them. Dora Tromanhauser, a former resident of White Bluffs, responded to Edmund Anderson's letter asking for permission to move her parents' graves. In her letter, she told Anderson, "It all seems very hard to me. I would have thought that of all quiet restful places, White Bluffs would be, and then this. This is most surely an uncertain old world."[48]

The resting place of the former residents of White Bluffs and Hanford at the Prosser Cemetery. The cemetery is one of the only reminders of the residents of the former towns. *Robert Bauman, January 2017*.

At least some former residents of the area saw, perhaps, a certain form of retribution in the moving of the settlers' graves. Former resident John McFee wrote Harry Anderson, Edmund's son, in 1976 in response to a request for stories about the towns in preparation for a reunion. In his letter, McFee told Anderson that his father's company had the contract to build the rail line from Beverly to Hanford. The planned line would go through a small Indian burial site. According to McFee, "the graves were moved over the Indian protests. Their spokesman at that time said, 'We have no power to stop you, but if you do this, the white man will live to see the day when his graves will be moved and he, like us, will be powerless to prevent it.'" Whether an actual occurrence or apocryphal story, to McFee and others it helped explain what had happened to their family members. And it also reflected a reality of life for Native peoples in the Americas for hundreds of years—the removal, destruction, and desecration of their ancestors' graves and burial sites.[49]

Indeed, Native peoples within the area to be taken for the Hanford Site also faced forced evacuation, as they had experienced throughout the previous two hundred years on the American continent. The small Wanapum tribe that resided in the Priest Rapids Valley had not signed a treaty with the federal government, and as a result, had not been placed on a reservation. But the Wanapum, whose name is believed to mean "distant" or "people at the end or the extremity," moved to different areas

The Buck family, members of the Wanapum people, who were forced to leave their traditional homelands in the Priest Rapids Valley to make room for the Hanford Engineer Works. *Hanford History Project, Harry and Juanita Anderson Collection, RG41_1349.*

in the region depending on the season, living at Priest Rapids during the winter. As Wanapum member Frank Buck, who was sixteen years old in 1943, remembered in 1984, "when the Army came into Hanford they said we can't go in there [Priest Rapids]. Some years when this is all over, you can come back and fish again whenever you want to. But, now we can't do that." Indeed, the Manhattan Engineer District (MED) did initially allow Wanapum members to maintain their fishing rights, even after they were prohibited from living within the boundaries of the Hanford Site. Eventually, the MED refused to allow even that access for the Wanapum, and continued a long history of federal removal of Native peoples from their traditional lands. Like the white residents of the communities in the Priest Rapids Valley, the Wanapum had also lost their land and their spaces and places of meaning.[50]

Almost simultaneously with the removal of residents from the Priest Rapids Valley, the federal government forced Japanese Americans, two-thirds of whom were citizens of the United States, to leave their homes and face imprisonment in internment camps often thousands of miles from their homes. Unlike the white residents of the Priest Rapids Valley, Japanese Americans did not receive any compensation or appraisal value from the government. Most were forced to sell their homes, businesses, and farms at cut-rate prices. Many lost virtually everything. Compensation for Japanese Americans would not come until decades later, long after many of the original prisoners had died. Like the pre-1943 residents of Richland, White Bluffs, and Hanford, Japanese Americans had been forced to move due to a "wartime necessity." But that is where the similarities end. Japanese-Americans were imprisoned and would receive no compensation for their land and property for decades. Even then, it never came close to matching what they had lost.[51]

Japanese-American families in the Hanford region too faced removal. The War Relocation Authority determined that the Columbia River would serve as the dividing line for the internment of Japanese Americans. Residents of Japanese descent in Franklin County, where Pasco was located, did not face imprisonment, but residents of Japanese descent in Benton County, where Kennewick and Richland were located, were imprisoned. For instance, members of the Yamauchi family, long-time residents of the area who lived in Benton County, were interned; family members who lived in Franklin County, for the most part, were not interned.[52]

For decades, the towns of Hanford and White Bluffs remained largely forgotten, except by the former residents who gathered every year at Howard Amon Park in Richland to reminisce, and by the occasional newspaper reporter who wrote a story about the towns. Those stories would put the towns and their former residents briefly in the spotlight, only to fade again into the background of history.

The reasoning behind the origins of both the Hanford Oral History Project and the Hanford History Project was to ensure that those people, Native and white, and those towns would not disappear into historical oblivion. Dick Wiehl summed up the feelings of many of the former residents of White Bluffs and Hanford in his oral history interview in 2013. When asked about the importance of the town of White Bluffs, Wiehl replied: "Right now, it's forgotten. And, that doesn't seem to be fair." And Wiehl added that making a history of White Bluffs "may also help bring closure to a lot of the people that are content that their story has been told."[53] Perhaps the stories of the former residents of these communities and their memories of their forced evacuation from those spaces and places of meaning will help preserve the memories of those towns and their former residents and help us better understand the lives and experiences of those who lived in the rural American West.

Those memories demonstrate that the former residents of the region, both Native American and white, were more than helpless victims of an aggressive federal government. That often has been the narrative about those communities. Instead many of these residents proactively challenged government appraisals, and in the long run received more compensation for the loss of their land. Others insisted on the removal of cemeteries so they could visit the graves of their loved ones, or in the case of the Wanapum, insisted on the appropriate marking of them as important cultural sites. Still others eventually worked at the Hanford Site during World War II and/or the Cold War, often driving past the places where they and their families had lived, worked, and established communities. Those former residents often felt as though they were making a second contribution to America's war efforts. All of the former residents of the

Hanford region negotiated and navigated the changes wrought by the war, adapted the best they could, and tried to come to terms with their lost places and spaces of meaning.

Notes

1. For years this building had been known as the Bruggemann warehouse, the assumption being that it had been a fruit storage warehouse. Paula Bruggemann disputed that notion in her oral history interview, and convincingly argued that it was, indeed, a cookhouse. Paula Bruggemann Holm, interview by Robert Bauman, Hanford History Project (HHP), August 6, 2014, Yakima, Washington.

2. For more on Indian removal and reservation policy, see Richard White, *"It's Your Misfortune and None of My Own": A New History of the American West* (Norman: University of Oklahoma Press, 1991), especially chapter 4.

3. Annette Heriford, interview by S. L. Sanger, 1984, quoted in Sanger, *Working on the Bomb: An Oral History of WWII Hanford* (Portland State University, 1995), 21.

4. Quoted in "Hanford Stirs Bitter Memories 50 Years Later," *Salem Statesman Journal,* February 14, 1993.

5. W. Jerome Clarke, memoir, East Benton County Historical Society and Museum, (EBCHSM).

6. Walter Grisham, interview by Ellen Prendergast, Hanford Cultural Resources Laboratory Oral History Program (HCRL), August 6, 2001; Pacific Northwest National Laboratory, *The Hanford and White Bluffs Agricultural Landscape: Evaluation for Listing in the National Register of Historic Places* (September 2003), 39.

7. Gordon Kaas, interview by Robert Bauman, HHP, June 12, 2013.

8. Robert Fletcher, interview by Robert Bauman, HHP, August 20, 2013.

9. Ray Deranleau, interview by Robert Bauman, HHP, September 3, 2013.

10. Nancy Mendenhall, *Orchards of Eden: White Bluffs on the Columbia, 1907–1943* (Seattle: Far Eastern Press, 2006), 407.

11. Lloyd Wiehl, interview by S. L. Sanger, 1984, quoted in Sanger, *Working on the Bomb,* 25.

12. Kathleen Hitchcock, interview by S. L. Sanger, 1984, quoted in Sanger, *Working on the Bomb,* 22–23.

13. Sally Brown Gonzales to Alene Clarke, March 27, 2000, EBCHSM.

14. Catherine Borden Finley, interview by Robert Bauman, HHP, July 9, 2013.

15. Ibid.

16. Ibid.

17. Ibid; "Richland Folk Will Conduct Own Appraisal," *Kennewick Courier*, April 10, 1943.

18. Jack Collins, interview by Robert Bauman, HHP, August 4, 2013.

19. Ibid.

20. Mendenhall, 416.

21. Lee Ann Powell, "Culture, Cold War, Conservatism, and the End of the Atomic Age; Richland, Washington, 1943–1989" (PhD diss., Washington State University, 2013), 36–37.

22. Jay Perry, "Land Confiscations," EBCHSM, Hanford File.

23. Bone to Wheeler, April 13, 1943. Quoted in Mendenhall, p. 408.

24. War Department Report, May 1944, Harry and Juanita Anderson Collection, Box 3, Folder A8, HHP.

25. Ibid.

26. Ibid.

27. Ben and Elise Moede Appraisal documents, July 6, 1943, Harry and Juanita Anderson Collection, Box 1, Folder 17, HHP.

28. "Richland Folk Will Conduct Own Appraisal," *Kennewick Courier*, April 10, 1943; Jay Perry, "Land Confiscations," EBCHSM.

29. Robert Fletcher interview.

30. Gordon Kaas interview.

31. "Richland Folk Will Conduct Own Appraisal."

32. Lloyd Chalcraft, interview by Robert Bauman, HHP, August 20, 2013.

33. Ibid.

34. "Hanford Stirs Bitter Memories 50 Years Later."

35. Heriford interview, Sanger, 21.

36. Mendenhall, 411–16.

37. Ibid.

38. "Use of Pressure Charged in Hanford Land Seizures," *Seattle Times*, December 18, 1944.

39. Yvonne and Dale McGee, interview by Ellen Prendergast, HCRL Oral History Project, July 11, 2001.

40. Ibid.

41. "Number of Hanford Evacuations Would Disturb Service Sons, Farmer Charges," *Seattle Times*, December 19, 1944.

42. Dick Wiehl, interview by Robert Bauman, HHP, June 5, 2013.

43. Claude Rawlins, interview by Robert Bauman, HCRL, October 1, 2000.

44. Chalcraft interview.

45. "Final Report on Removal of Cemeteries in Hanford Engineer Works Project," War Department, June 1944, Harry and Juanita Anderson Collection, Box 10, Folder 6, HHP.

46. "White Bluffs Cemetery Moved to Prosser," *Prosser Record-Bulletin*, May 18, 1944. See also, J. E. Leander, White Bluffs Cemetery Association Meeting Notes, May 1, 1943; Fred Johnston, War Department to Edmund Anderson, June 3, 1943; and Norman Fuller, War Department to Edmund Anderson, May 29, 1944; all Harry and Juanita Anderson Collection, Box 10, Folder 6, HHP.

47. Harry Anderson letter to Prosser Cemetery Association, printed in *Prosser Record-Bulletin*, May 18, 1944.

48. Dora Tromanhauser to Edmund Anderson, May 29, 1943, Harry and Juanita Anderson Collection, Box 10, Folder 6, HHP.

49. John McFee to Harry Anderson, June 24, 1976, Harry and Juanita Anderson Collection, Box 4, Folder 1, HHP.

50. Frank Buck, interview with S. L. Sanger, 1984, quoted in Sanger, *Working on the Bomb*, 26. See also, Powell, 27–31; White, chapter 4.

51. Erika Lee, *The Making of Asian America: A History* (New York: Simon and Schuster, 2015), 211–51.

52. Andrew Sirocchi, "Members of Pioneering Family Celebrate Their Heritage in Pasco," *Tri-City Herald*, August 14, 2005.

53. Dick Wiehl interview.

$ 669, 266 B

$ 5,272,645

$ 669, 266

$ 5,370,097

CHAPTER FIVE

Hanford and White Bluffs Reunions

Remembering the Pre-War Communities of the Priest Rapids Valley

Robert Bauman and Robert Franklin

Former residents of the Priest Rapids Valley continued to gather annually to picnic and keep the sense of community together after eviction, although in two different organizations. From 1943 to 1967, former Hanford and White Bluffs residents picnicked on the first Sunday in August in Prosser and at some point formed the White Bluffs-Hanford Pioneer Association. Beginning in 1968 they established formalized, full-fledged annual reunions. Indeed, a yearly newsletter advertised the reunions, which included tours of the site and a picnic at Howard Amon Park along the Columbia River in Richland. The picnic featured photo displays, trivia games, and dancing among other events. The organizers Annette Heriford and Harry Anderson (son of Edmund Anderson) produced short songs and skits based on the collective memories of community members (assisted by family reminiscences and questionnaires solicited every year), cajoled former residents on their mailing list to attend the annual gatherings, and advertised events like the "Sagebrush Shuffle" for their VIPs—"Very Important Pioneers."[1] Throughout its existence, the association gathered physical materials such as diaries, photographs, and documents to create a locus of memory, for they had been alienated from their lands by eminent domain. The family of Harry Anderson donated the records of the White Bluffs-Hanford Pioneer Association to the Hanford History Project in 2016.

One of the authors of this chapter, Robert Bauman, first met and interviewed some of the former residents of Hanford and White Bluffs at their annual reunion picnic in the year 2000. By that time, the annual picnics had brought family members and friends back together for decades to reminisce about their previous lives and those communities long since gone. Those annual gatherings were both inclusive—spouses, children, grandchildren, and family friends were all welcome—and exclusive—former residents of Richland who were forced to leave their homes were not invited to these gatherings. Instead, residents of Richland held their own reunion known as the Old Timers' Picnic with a similar aim—to keep alive the memory of the displaced community. It is unknown exactly why the displaced persons formed two distinct reunion associations, but the answer may lie, in part, in how the communities interacted when they were existent. Hanford and White Bluffs were on the rail line from Beverly, whereas Richland was closer to Kennewick and Pasco. More likely, though, were the somewhat different experiences of the residents of the various towns. While some Richlanders had to leave their homes, White Bluffs and Hanford reunion organizers reasoned, their town remained standing. The reunions for both groups were well attended until the mid-1990s when attendance began to slip as the original residents began to pass away. The White Bluffs-Hanford Pioneer Association last met in 2005, Heriford passed away in 2009, and the Old Timers' Picnic ended around that time as well, although some former Richland residents continued to meet less formally at a local restaurant.

By 2000, Heriford was the key driving force behind continuing the reunions, and she was the first person Bauman met when he began conducting interviews of former residents for a cultural resources management project for the Pacific Northwest National Laboratory (PNNL). Heriford was a bundle of energy and determination. She had a chip on her shoulder from what had happened to Hanford and White Bluffs, and she wanted everyone she met to know about the sacrifices residents of those towns had made for the war effort. She remained angry and bitter over the way her family was treated and nostalgic for her family farm that had been just a memory for decades by 2000. For Heriford, the annual reunions were a way to stay connected or reconnect with Hanford in the years before the war. For Heriford and others at the reunions, the Priest

Rapids Valley in the years before the war was an enchanting place in a magical time.

But while the town of Hanford may have seemed like a magical place to a young Annette Heriford, in many ways it was anything but special or magical. Indeed, Hanford and White Bluffs were quite typical rural towns in eastern Washington and in the semi-arid intermountain American West. Like people in many similar towns constructed in the early

1968 White Bluffs-Hanford Pioneer Association reunion at the White Bluffs ferry landing. *Hanford History Project, Harry and Juanita Anderson Collection, RG4I_1724.*

twentieth century, Hanford and White Bluffs residents worked hard just to survive. The intense dry heat of the summer, the cold and winds of the winter, the devastating economic impact of the Great Depression—all made life in these towns physically, economically, and at times, emotionally challenging, and anything but magical or wonderful or special.

But for many former residents, romanticizing those towns in the years before the war helped them make sense of what had happened to those communities. Creating exclusive reunions helped preserve that sense of

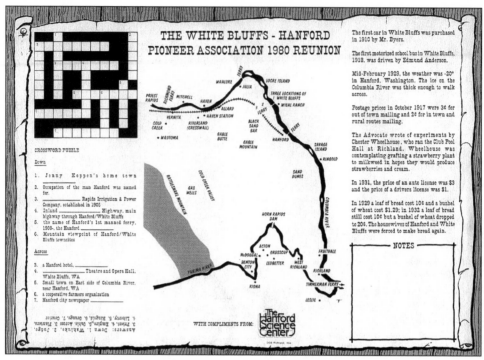

Inside page of the program for the White Bluffs-Hanford Pioneer Association 1980 Reunion. The crossword puzzle clues reinforced the closed nature of the group. *Hanford History Project, Harry and Juanita Anderson Collection, Box 14, Folder 4.*

belonging to a special group. The programs and activities at the annual reunions often reflected that need for feeling connected to a special, unique place and group of people. For instance, the clues for the cross-word puzzle in the 1980 reunion materials could only be answered by a former resident of White Bluffs or Hanford—someone with intimate knowledge of those communities and the people who had lived there. Non-residents were unlikely to know the name of the hotel in Hanford or the newspaper printed there. Indeed, the former residents of Hanford and White Bluffs clearly saw themselves as members of a special club—one whose members had shared a unique and traumatic experience that others could not fully understand.

Leatris Reed attended some of these reunions and went on one of the tours of the former town sites. She recalled: "it broke my heart...there wasn't any stumps of trees left. There wasn't anything left."[2] For some, the reunions were a time to mourn the loss of a special place; for others they were a time to deepen emotional bonds and tell personal stories that may not have come out if the community was intact. Robert Fletcher met an old neighbor, Bruce Frasier, at an Old Timers' Picnic and learned that when Frasier's father died during the Depression, Fletcher's parents provided food and cash assistance to help the widow and her three children.[3] The reunions provided myriad ways for former residents to make emotional connections to their collective and individual pasts.

The efforts that residents went through to memorialize their communities speaks to the importance of a sense of place, one that was altered but not destroyed by the evacuations in 1943. Again, the reunion programs provide evidence of that often romanticized sense of place. For example, the cover of the 1980 Reunion Program featured a photograph of the check dam and fishing platform at Horn Rapids on the Yakima River. In this image, the region is the peaceful, idyllic rural West that many former residents chose to remember. It is difficult to imagine, when looking at this photograph, that this idyllic world would end so abruptly and that residents would be uprooted to make room for a wartime project focused on ultimate violence and destruction.

While the 1980 program recalled the idyllic, rural West, the cover of the 1988 program reflected another common theme emphasized by former White Bluffs and Hanford residents—that of the harsh pioneer life and the promises of that life dashed. Indeed, the name of the organization—the White Bluffs-Hanford Pioneer Association—and the members' practice of referring to themselves as VIPs—"Very Important Pioneers"—demonstrated their self-identity as pioneers of the old West. At the same time, the wagon wheel on the cover has fallen into disrepair, reflecting both the rugged life of western pioneers and the devastation of dreams unfulfilled and communities long gone.

Finally, the cover of the 1990 reunion program combines both the theme of a pastoral, rural West, and the notion of rugged pioneers. The image of the horse and buggy calls forth both an older, simpler time before

White Bluffs-Hanford Annual Reunion Program, 1980. The photo emphasized the group's perception of themselves as rural pioneers. *Hanford History Project, Harry and Juanita Anderson Collection, Box 14, Folder 4.*

automobiles, and the idea of a pioneer lifestyle. The windmill, farmhouse, and farm buildings further evoke the notion of a simpler, rural existence that was no longer attainable. Each of these three reunion program covers romanticized the lost, rural American West in general, and for attendees of the annual picnics in particular, brought back memories of the literal ghost towns of Hanford and White Bluffs. The covers were, indeed, images of a bygone past that could no longer be recaptured.

At one of the annual reunions, the family of Edmund Anderson— Ellen, Clarene, Arthur, and Harry—showed a film about the town sites to the former residents of those towns. The film included images of community events and farms and buildings that no longer existed. Along with the film, the Anderson family composed a brief prologue for the guests to read before watching the film. Titled "In Retrospect," the prologue romanticized the lost towns and dedicated the film to be shown to people of the Priest Rapids Valley, "to their work on the long sunburnt slopes of the west where the communities of White Bluffs and Hanford were born in dreams and obliterated by history." The prologue informed the film viewers and former residents that they would see "only the physical fragments of what was in this valley...the orchards, the schools, the community band, the people who were here and are no longer." But what the viewers could not see were "the dreams that lived in this valley and that remain in the hearts of those who remember."[4]

This cover of the 1988 White Bluffs-Hanford Reunion Program highlights both the pioneer identity of the former residents and the difficulties of farming in the Priest Rapids Valley. *Hanford History Project, Harry and Juanita Anderson Collection, Box 14, Folder 4.*

1943 -- WHITE BLUFFS-HANFORD 47TH ANNUAL REUNION -- 1990

The cover of the 1990 White Bluffs-Hanford Reunion Program featured an idyllic rural past celebrated by the former residents of the Priest Rapids Valley. *Hanford History Project, Harry and Juanita Anderson Collection, Box 14, Folder 4.*

It has been only natural for former residents of Hanford and White Bluffs over the years to talk of dreams unfulfilled and to wonder what might have been. Former Hanford resident Donald Evett years later said he often wondered how, "had it not been for the Manhattan Project that came here, perhaps Hanford and White Bluffs would have developed into some of the finest fruit-growing country." As Walt Grisham wistfully noted, residents of these towns lost their neighbors and their communities and their roots. The evacuation "destroyed some dreams," he said. "We didn't get the chance to change like the rest of the country did. We didn't have the chance to do that…. How can you measure what might have been?"[5] For Evett and Grisham and many others who hailed from the

Priest Rapids Valley of eastern Washington, attempting to measure what might have been for the towns of White Bluffs and Hanford proved futile.

What could be measured was what had been accomplished. Dozens of families had carved farms, orchards, and towns out of the dry, scrub brush of eastern Washington. They had built their own irrigation lines, initially with vitrified clay piping, in order to produce bounties of crops that were just beginning to bring a profit to many when the war came. And they had built communities of people connected to each other and their lost places strongly enough to bring them together year after year along the river in the desert to celebrate what had been and what they had been able to measure.

Notes

1. Harry and Juanita Anderson Collection, Box 14, Folder 1, Hanford History Project (HHP), Washington State University Tri-Cities.

2. Leatris Reed, interview by Robert Bauman, HHP, August 28, 2013.

3. Robert Fletcher, interview by Robert Bauman, HHP, August 20, 2013.

4. "In Retrospect," Harry and Juanita Anderson Collection, HHP, Washington State University Tri-Cities.

5. Walter Grisham, interview by Ellen Prendergast, HCRL, August 6, 2001; Donald Evett, quoted in Pacific Northwest National Laboratory, *Hanford and White Bluffs Agricultural Landscape*, 39.

Oral History Interviews

Introduction

Robert Bauman

Nowhere to Remember is based largely on oral histories completed as part of the Hanford Oral History Project and the Hanford History Project. Those oral histories have formed the basis of the chapters, highlighting their events and themes, but the chapters include only pieces and slices of those oral histories. The editors felt the reader would appreciate a sampling of full oral interview transcripts to learn how we conducted the interviews and what types of questions we asked. We also thought that the reader might want to see fuller and more complete responses than are included in the text, and read about other events, happenings, and memories that, for various reasons, were left out of the text.

We have chosen to include the transcripts of Robert Fletcher, Leatris Reed, and Dick Wiehl, in part because they offer some of the more complete and detailed accounts of life in the pre-1943 Priest Rapids Valley. Also, they provide a good representation of the interviews in terms of content and life experiences. The families of Robert Fletcher and Dick Wiehl were still living in the area at the time of the evacuation in 1943; Leatris Reed's family had left the area two years earlier. Fletcher's and Wiehl's interviews furnish some of the better descriptions of the evacuation and its impact on families in area. Reed and Fletcher deliver richly detailed accounts of life in the region during the Great Depression. Reed's interview also brings a woman's perspectives and experiences. Wiehl and Reed, in particular, were some of the best storytellers that we interviewed. Reading the complete transcripts of their interviews takes the reader back to the small towns of the region in the 1930s and 1940s. Each of these interviews gives the reader a good sense of the personality or flavor of the individual, and you can sense the emotions they felt in recalling their lives in these spaces and places of memory.

Finally, we want to inform readers that the transcripts of each of these three interviews, as well as all of the interviews that comprise the Hanford Oral History Project, can be viewed on the Hanford History Project website at www.hanfordhistory.com. We encourage interested readers to further explore other interviews there.

Robert Fletcher, on Richland

Interview conducted by Robert Bauman, August 20, 2013,
campus of Washington State University Tri-Cities

Robert Fletcher

BAUMAN: Okay, let's start by having you say your name.

FLETCHER: I'm Robert Fletcher.

BAUMAN: Thank you. So let's start, if we could, by maybe having you talk about your family and how they came to this area, what brought them here, when they came—that sort of thing.

FLETCHER: My folks—my mother and father—grew up in Wisconsin. They knew each other in high school, and my father came out west because my mother had relatives in Idaho, and after she graduated she came out here to stay with them and go to business college in Spokane. So my dad was fond of her and he followed her by working his way west. He was an expert milker, and he could always get a job in a dairy. Because when you worked in a dairy milking cows you had to get up at 3:00 in the morning. And so when he'd work his way from Wisconsin to maybe South Dakota, and he would see—in the depot, in the train depot—he would look on the bulletin board for openings for milkers and he always found work. And he could stay there for several weeks till he got enough money to move on. So he wound up in Lewiston, Idaho, I believe it was. And eventually he and my mother got together and they got married in Coeur d'Alene, [Idaho,] 1912. And I had a sister born in 1915 in Coeur d'Alene, Francille. And another sister was born in 1918. In the meantime, during World War I, my dad had been working in a, what's called electrical

substation in Coeur d'Alene. And during the war then he went over to
Bremerton and worked in the shipyards at Bremerton, wiring electrical wiring
on the ships. And my mother eventually followed. My mother became a
secretary and could do the office work. But after kids were born, she didn't do
much of that. And then after the war was over, Bremerton jobs closed up and
he went back to work at another electric substation down by Walla Walla,
Milton-Freewater. And he had been raised on a farm and he had a desire to
be independent. So at that time there were developments in Kennewick and
the whole Tri-City area. They were developed because irrigation water was
being made available from the rivers. And in Richland, there were private
developers and they would get bonds that were backed by the state. The
state government wanted to support the development to get started, and that
was in late 1918s, '20s. And I'm sure my dad—well, my dad told me that
there were brochures that these companies would advertise that, come to
Kennewick or Richland, that water was available, the climate was ideal, and
their soil was great, and you could make a living on just a few acres if you
knew how to farm. So my dad traveled out here. His name was Francis, and
C. F. Fletcher was his—And he bought 20 acres of sagebrush. It was what is
now on—what did I say?

BAUMAN: Spangler?

FLETCHER: Spangler Road. He bought 20 acres there out there at the top
of the hill. It was all sagebrush. And then later he bought 10 acres down
below the hill where there now is a trailer park or mobile homes. He had
to arrange to get the teams of horses to pull out the sagebrush and level the
ground. My mother and—I believe that she had two children then, Francille,
and Medo is my other sister's name, born in 1918. They came out by train
from Walla Walla to Kennewick. And Morton Hess met them at—Morton
Hess had a improvised old pickup that dad said that they met them at the
depot in Kennewick, and he brought them out to the farmhouse he'd rented.
Before that, my dad had a team of horses, and he brought all his possessions
in a wagon from Milton-Freewater to Richland that took him three days,
he said, to make that trip with the team of horses. And so after he got the
house rented, then he sent for my mother, had my mother come out with the
children. And they lived in this rented farmhouse about a quarter of a mile
away. And there were a few other houses, a few other farms being developed
at the same time. So that took a lot of effort. It was 1920, and he told me
that he had to put in the irrigation. The company brought water to the edge
of your property and then you had to put in the pipe yourself. They were

cement pipes, about three feet long, 40 pounds, eight inches in diameter. And he said he put in several hundred feet of this pipe and he thought he'd done a pretty good job. He worked hard. Turned the water on and it just leaked all over, so he had to do it all over again. He was pretty persistent. And then they had a hard time the first few years because he was small, a small person, and a greenhorn. About the only income work you could get then was to work for the irrigation company if you wanted to earn some money. And usually that was when the water was shut off and they had to clean and repair the ditches, open ditches. And he said they wouldn't hire him for a year or two because they thought well, he was a greenhorn. He wouldn't last anyway, and he was kind of small. But he stuck it out. And what happened was they had to put in some new pumps for the irrigation system, and these were larger pumps. They were three-phase motors, and there wasn't anybody immediately around that knew how to fix them, how to hook them up. Excuse me, I get very emotional. So he told them he thought he thought he could do it. He wasn't too sure. He said he could do it. He told them he could do it. He said he, personally, he said he wasn't too sure. But anyway, he went ahead with it and they worked fine. And after that, he said he didn't have any trouble getting a job for the irrigation district. And later on, several years after he got the farm started and everything, he did become manager of the irrigation district. When I talk about the irrigation district, it wasn't a huge one, but there was about 5,000 acres under water. And most of the farms were like ours, 20, 30 acres. And because you had to have a team of horses. You couldn't farm like you can nowadays with everything mechanized like it is. Lots of hand labor. So I was born in 1922, and I believe that they were still in this rented house. But in the meantime, they'd begun work on a basement, which was about half underground and half above ground with concrete side walls. And so it was above the ground enough, it had had fairly good sized windows. And there were just two rooms. The total probably wasn't more than 40 feet long and 20 feet wide. And above that they put a temporary sort of a shelter that was more of a tent house with a wooden roof and canvas with a wooden frame with canvas around it. And that was our bedroom. That was where we had our bedrooms. And it was cold in the winter and hot in the summer, but in the summertime you could roll the canvas up and the evening breeze would cool it off. In the wintertime we had feather beds and my mother would warm up hot irons on the cook stove, and we'd wrap them in towels and put in our beds. And we managed, thought we were living all right. There wasn't any bathroom—there was no indoor bathroom, no indoor water supply. He dug a well down below the hill. Had to do it by hand, about 20 feet deep. And the way to get water up to the house, he had a, we called it a stone boat, it was a sled. He hooked the horses to it, the sled, and two pretty good sized barrels, I suppose 40 gallon barrels or something. He'd fill them with water from the hand pump down below the hill. And he'd circle around it, bring that sled up. That was the water supply for a few days. But of course, it didn't always last long enough. And I can remember my mother carrying two buckets of water up the hill. Excuse me. [*emotional*] It was a hard life for women, especially, carrying water up the hill, and all the other work they had to do then. She was in charge of the garden. Of course, we had our weekly bath by a copper tub on a cook stove. And the tub, and that's where we took our weekly bath, and shared the affair. The two rooms in the house were the kitchen and then where we ate. The other room was the living quarters and where somebody might sleep if they were not feeling well, otherwise we slept upstairs in the tent house. So those were the early days. It took them quite a little while for my dad to get established, and also get some crops down that they could pay for their living expenses. And they had Fresnos then that the team of horses would pull, and they'd scoop the dirt and dump it in the low places and level it out. And farmers worked together on that. I can remember our neighbors—as I said, most people lived within a quarter or a half mile of each other. The Barnetts and the Nickolauses lived close to us and we shared—when it was time to put in some of the crops, the Barnetts would come with their mowing machine and there would be two or three mowing machines and everything going on, and we'd go back and forth and get the job done.

BAUMAN: So what sorts of crops did you grow then?

FLETCHER: We—it was truck farming. We had to raise—we had to have cows. Truck farming was not too reliable. You had to, to fall back on, you had a herd of cow—most all farmers had a herd of cattle which they had milk cows and some beef cows. And you milked the cow—you had your own milking and made your own cheese, but you could sell to the creamery in Kennewick. And we had a milk house where we'd separate the cream from the milk. And we had the Twin City Dairy, I think it was, would come by once a week and collect the milk. We'd keep the milk in a cool water place or something. I don't remember now in details. We didn't have refrigeration. Maybe they came back twice a week. I'm not sure. So we had a herd of cattle, and of course you always had a team of work horses. And I had a pony when I got old enough, about third grade I think. In school I got a pony that had been tamed—he had been one of the wild horses from Horse Heaven Hills. And a bunch of horses had been caught. And we bought it from another fella, and he was a real—Shorty was his name, and I thought he was the greatest horse, because he could outrun any horse. We had horse races. And a lot of the kids, the only horse they had to ride was a work horse. So I was very fortunate. Anyway, we raised alfalfa for the cattle and the animals. Alfalfa and clover, and of course you had to mow the hay in the summertime and let it dry and put it up in wagons and carry it and take it into the hay stack for the winter. We also raised some acres of corn, of field corn, although we could eat some of the corn when it was quite young, but it was mostly raised for the cattle. And we had an in-ground silo where we had a—we'd bring in, when the corn was mature we'd cut it down with machetes and bring the corn stocks and ears and all and run it through the chopper and made silage out of it. It would ferment in this silo, which was about 20 feet deep and it was dug out near the barnyard. And about I guess 12 feet wide or so. As a kid it looked bigger, probably, than it actually was. But anyway, that was part of the barnyard. And with the silage and the haystack, we kept the cattle going through the winter. Because you had to have enough hay to get through and that took quite a load. And then for field crops, we had a cherry orchard of three or four acres. We raised asparagus three or four acres. And that was a job that—that was a cash crop that came on early in the year in March. And the whole family pitched in. We got up early, almost daybreak to cut the asparagus. Before school you had to have it cut. And then they'd go ahead and you had to pack it in crates to get it ready to go to market. So we had the asparagus, and then we had, between the trees in the orchard—one time my dad experimented with peanuts. And I don't think they turned out too well because I don't remember him having them very long. We planted strawberries. We had strawberries that we picked after the asparagus was done, the strawberries would be ripe. And then the cherries would get ripe in June usually. And so it was staggered out. And then we always had a field of potatoes that you'd dig with a team or horses and a digger. But before you did that, you had to get seed potatoes, and they came whole. The family would—we had a cellar in our house. We'd cut those potatoes into quarters, so there's an eye on each one and that would sprout into a potato plant. And we spent probably a couple weeks, maybe not that long, cutting the seed potatoes into where they could be planted in the field. And I'm trying to think of other crops that we had. I know he tried different ones. We had peas—peas in a pod. And I don't think that paid off too well because I don't remember it lasting too long. Oh, we had some peaches. Not a big orchard, but we had some peaches and apricot trees. Those were sort of under my mother's domain, the garden and the apricots. And she made sure that we all pitched in and helped do the weeding and planting and picking. And all of that had to be picked and canned for the winter. I can remember my mother and sisters working hard—doing a lot of work canning. And the cellar was just full of—they were quite proud to display, in those days, to display their glass jars of fruit, peaches and everything. And took it to the fair to see if they could win some blue ribbons. So we didn't buy too much from the local grocery store, except cooking oil and bananas—fruit that wouldn't grow here. Orange. Those were a treat. Just a few times during the year bananas and oranges we got at Christmastime or your birthday or something. And the store was John Dam's, John Dam Plazas down here, named after the Dam Grocery Store. And there were two men, John Dam and Victor Nelson. They ran the grocery store. And you didn't go looking for your things. You handed them a list. You wanted two gallons of kerosene for your lamps and lanterns that you needed. No electric lights. And as I said, cooking oil, and flour and sugar in bulk. And once in a while you'd get a treat of candy or something such as that. So I think that covers pretty much what the farm was like.

BAUMAN: The crops that you grew, the cherries, strawberries, did you sell those somewhere?

FLETCHER: Yeah. We picked and put them in crates. There was what they called the Big Y—it was in Kennewick. And it stood for Yakima I think. Yakima—there was a branch of Yakima Produce Company. And later on I worked there nailing, making boxes for different kinds of fruit when I was in high school.

BAUMAN: Mm-hm.

FLETCHER: In fact, most kids did extra jobs like that. Excuse me. I've got to take a drink.

BAUMAN: Sure.

FLETCHER: All right.

BAUMAN: I was going to ask you about your farm. You mentioned some underground silo. Were there any other buildings on your farm? Any warehouse or barn or any of that sort of thing?

FLETCHER: Yeah. There was a barn from the cows, of course. And there are pictures in my booklet of some of these chicken houses in the yard, a couple of chicken houses. And a milk house. We had pigs. The pigs consumed a lot of the excess milk. You could—they'd eat most anything you had that was extra. And that was another thing we shared was when it came time to butcher a cow or a calf or a pig for meat, there was a man that was sort of a local veterinarian—I don't think he had a degree—Sam Supplee. If your horse got sick, he knew what—or an animal got his foot caught in the barbed wire, he knew how to treat it. And he'd come by. And he also knew how to butcher animals quite well. And he would come out. And I can remember that we had a hole, a pit dug out where we could put a fire in there, and it was covered with some kind of bars or metal affair. And a vat of water would be put in that over the fire at ground level. And adjacent to that would be a platform where the pig was killed. And after it had been killed and the organs taken out, they'd roll it into that vat of boiling water and then pull it back out again after a few minutes. Then you could scrape the bristles off of the pig. And Sam Supplee then would do the rest of the butchering. They'd hang it up to cure overnight, and then to cut it up. And for his efforts, he'd get part of the meat, or other people that had helped out, and that's the way that they operated. And he was a local person they turned to. There were other veterinarians in Pasco or Kennewick, but he was the one that they mainly relied on. Our horses, we had two work horses, Star and Monte. I can remember them well, and that was one of my jobs when I got home from school, after, was usually to rub them down after a day's work in the field, because they'd be all sweaty. Or on days when I wasn't at school, too, in the summertime, to take them down to the ditch where they'd drink a lot of water. They got real hot and sweaty. And then take the harnesses off. And there's lots of preparation before you could do too much. And so those were some of my jobs was to take in—you got home from school, the first thing to do was take in the firewood for the wood stove or the heating stove. And there were plenty of other things to do around the barnyard, to clean out the stall, or clean out the barn and see that horses were fed and such things as that.

BAUMAN: Mm-hm.

FLETCHER: The thing was, I think that maybe a little different than nowadays, kids knew that they were part of the family and that they were an important part of the family. And that they had jobs to do. And just it was the thing that made families close.

BAUMAN: Sure.

FLETCHER: I wanted to mention, too, that we did have special family friends. I mentioned the Barnetts. And they had kids that were—Dan Barnett was about my age. And my sisters had—they had daughters. Anyway, they had kids about our same age. The Hackneys were another family that lived not very far away and had a farm. And there was Richard Hackney and Dan Barnett and I were always good friends for a long time. And some other kids in that area, the Supplees. So I guess I forgot where I was here. The Hackneys and the Fletcher families and the Carlsons were particularly close. The Carlsons also had children that were our ages. And we would get together for family picnics, and especially Fourth of July we'd make our homemade ice cream and take to Pasco Park where there'd be fireworks. And then in the summertime, we always had a break in the farm work of about four or five days where we could get away from the farm. Usually it was around the Fourth of July or a little bit after. And we would get away because the irrigation ditches were shut down for a few days, about four or five days in order for the ditches to dry out and the weeds could be cleaned out. Because they clogged up with moss and other stuff. So that they would dry out the ditches and we could get away from the farm, as long as we had a neighbor to take care of the animals that we had. And there were enough other people that would do that. We'd trade off. So we would manage to get away for about three or four days and go up to above Yakima, Naches and up into the woods. And we'd take our tents. One of the, the Hackneys, Art Hackney was a school bus driver, and school bus driver had to have their own buses. They'd own their own buses. So he could do with the bus whatever he wanted during the summertime. So he would be the one that we would load up the bus—he took a few of the seats out that could be taken out—with our camping gear in it, and some of the rest of the people would ride in that bus and others would go in their car. We'd invite some of our friends to go along too. So we'd have quite a group and several tents set up there around the lake up at Naches, Rimrock and up in that area. We had a wonderful time up in there with all our friends, and sitting around the campfire at night and hearing the stories that the older folks had to tell. So that's—

BAUMAN: Mm-hm. A real sense of community there, yeah.

FLETCHER: Yeah. Part of the community. It was a close-knit community for sure. And naturally, you had more close friends with some of the people than you did with others. But as I said in my book that there was no—when you were gone, nobody as I knew, locked their houses or worried about any of that sort of thing.

BAUMAN: Mm-hm. You mentioned earlier that the house you lived in there was no running water, right?

FLETCHER: Right.

BAUMAN: No electricity. Did you ever have a telephone?

FLETCHER: That's another little story. My mother, her relatives lived in Wallace, Idaho, and her uncle, aunt and uncle, her uncle was a master carpenter. And they were very close and would come down to visit us and they were very helpful. When we were, when my folks were just starting out, they were a backbone to help them out as much as they could. They bought eggs from them and they'd ship them. I have some letters that my mother saved of that period in time. You may be interested in some of those. Anyway, they would come down, and after my dad—after he had this basement house built, they was able to save up enough in about 10 years to—Josh Pentabaker was my uncle's, granduncle's name—was the main carpenter. And they arranged to buy a load of lumber from a lumber yard or a sawmill up in Bickleton, and they rented a truck or got somebody to haul this load of lumber down. And this Josh Pentabaker and my dad, and I think he got some local help, to get started on building a house above to replace that tent—actually a tent house that we had above the basement house. And then they enlarged it also. They made the basement twice as large to accommodate a more modern house. And that was in 1933 or 1934. And I think it was 1934 before we occupied it. And that included indoor bathroom and running water. In the meantime, before my dad was able to build a dig a new well up on top of the hill, he had to go down 60 feet for groundwater. And so that was quite a project. But he finally got it done. And he got an electric motor then. By that time, see, there was no electricity until during Roosevelt got the REA started, rural electricity or whatever the word is, REA. And you got an electric pump to pump the water up into a tank. And then you had pressure to run the water from the tank into the house—had water pressure. And so we had running water, we had an indoor bathroom, and those were quite appreciated. I think we got electric stove—that was one of the first things. And that was quite an improvement over a wood stove. Oh, and then there was. And he didn't have enough money, I don't believe—oh, let me tell you, or let me go back just a bit.

BAUMAN: Sure.

FLETCHER: Josh Pentabaker got this house pretty well built, but he had to go back and do his own work back in Wallace, Idaho. And my dad negotiated with a carpenter here, a local carpenter, Vandersant——he was a Dutchman. And my dad traded a cow, a milk cow for this fella to put in a—he was a master carpenter, too. He put in the kitchen cabinets, is what I'm trying to say, and some of the other cabinets in the bathroom and things like that in exchange for this cow. Now, there may have been other things involved, but that was the main thing. He told about that in later years, and I can vaguely remember. In addition to the basement then, we got a root cellar where we kept most of our things cold. But anyway, before he could get a refrigerator, he cut a hole in the wall of the kitchen and he made a cabinet inside, and hung outside a metal tank or a metal thing that held water. And then he ran down some gunnysack fabric and that wetted enough to evaporate and cool the cabinet inside. It was quite a contraption. But it worked enough that it probably wasn't much cooler than the basement, but anyway, it was up and it was handy. So that was when we—in 1934 I think that we occupied the house that's there now.

BAUMAN: Did you ever have a telephone during the time you were there?

FLETCHER: Yeah, we had a phone. You cranked it. I'm trying to think whether we had it when we lived in the basement, whether we had it there or not. It was a party line, and there would be three or four people on the same line. And you answered according to how many rings. If it was two rings it was yours, or a short and a long or something like that. And of course people listened in on what was going on. We had a crank—it was, you cranked it up in order to make the signal. And there was a main station downtown. We were three miles from the downtown area up on what is now George Washington Way. And what's the name of that street? I can't remember all those—the house was on—

BAUMAN: Spangler?

FLETCHER: Spangler, yeah. Spangler Road. We had to—you kept up—Dad kept up with what was available.

BAUMAN: Mm-hm. How about news? Was there a newspaper, or how did you learn about—

FLETCHER: There was. There was the *Benton County Advocate* came out once a week. In fact, I think I still have some copies of that somewhere. It was mostly local, of course. Somebody was entertaining a company from Wallace, Idaho or somewhere, or somebody was sick in the hospital. Ed Peddicord was the—as I remember, he was older than myself but younger than my parents, and he became the first postmaster when the Hanford project took over, and he was the postmaster for quite a few years before he retired from the Richland Post Office.

BAUMAN: I wanted to ask you about the school that you went to. Where was the school? Any memories you have?

FLETCHER: Okay, there were, in the downtown area of Richland, the—I'm trying to relate it to—the grade school went from grade one through grade eight. And it was two story with four classrooms on the bottom and four on the upper level. I think they had electric lights, as I remember. The floors were wood floors, and they treated them with oil before school was started and at Christmas vacation. So when you came back from school—they'd wipe them up, the oil—they'd treat the wood floors. They'd wipe up the oil before classes started, but there would still be all these spots left on it. And so we had to take our shoes off when we came home at night because we would track oil. That was just for a few weeks or for a week or two. And the stoves had a jacket around. Of course they were—I believe they were coal stove. And there would be a jacket around, a metal jacket around the outside to it, a couple of feet from the stove itself so the kids couldn't get up and get burned. But the jacket that surrounded them was probably three or four feet high, metal jacket. And we would—I remember hanging our white gloves things on that metal jacket to dry them out. And that was in the back of the room of course. That was your heat in the classroom. As I said, the bathrooms for boys and girls, most of them separate of course, were outside where you went out to the bathroom. And I don't recall any running water or anything in the—The other, the high school was, it wasn't torn down when the project started, Hanford project, right away. And it was built more—it had indoor bathrooms, was more up-to-date, more than the grade school, four levels. There are pictures of it in my booklet. So that was quite a step up.

BAUMAN: Do you remember any of the teachers from either school, or do you have any favorite teachers from that time?

FLETCHER: Oh yeah. I remember most of my teachers. My first grade teacher, Ms. Randolph, older lady. And she was very good. I can remember putting our mittens up around that canopy around the stove in the wintertime, put your mittens up to dry. And I can't offhand remember, but I can visualize most of my teachers. There was Mrs.—Miss Mallory—she was single then. Taught me in fourth grade. And there was Bill Rader, our eighth grade teacher. Kind of he was a pretty good disciplinarian. If people got out of line, he had a paddle that he didn't mind using. There was—I can't think of the names, really, offhand. And then of course, in the high school I remember more of the teachers that I had. The superintendent, he also taught a few classes in, because the grade school had one class of every grade level. I started in the first grade, I was five years old, and I became six in November. And the kids that I started with, about half of the 20—I think there were 20 in my graduating class—about half of them were the ones I started in first grade with. That's how permanent the group was. There was a lot of permanency. And we moved onto this—where each grade you had the same ones, you knew the people. There would be two or three changes each year. And so we knew each other very well. And the others I'd known quite well, too. My wife, she came later and joined when she was in about seventh or eighth grade I think, and she graduated too—I graduated in 1940 and she graduated in 1942. And in my graduating class there was 20, and hers there was only 12. I don't know why particularly. The high school, it was in freshman year you usually took typing and it pretty well diversified. History classes, English classes. I can remember the teachers, Mrs. Deighton and Mrs. Carmichael. She's the one that got very emotional when the kids acted up and would carry on. Mr. Carmichael was the superintendent, and Mr. Whitehead, rather. We had basketball teams. We played against—Kennewick and Pasco were out of our league. They were from too big a town. So we played Benton City. I played—even though I'm pretty short, I was on the basketball team. We didn't have a football team. We weren't big enough. [*laughter*] The high school was only—with four classes, probably only 80 students altogether. And so I was on the basketball team the last couple years anyway. And we would go up to—Hanford was about 20 miles upriver, and White Bluffs. They were a comparative size. And to Benton City, and also to Finley. We used to call it Riverview then. It was a comparative size to what we were in Richland at that time. So we had a group that we played softball league and basketball. No football that I can remember.

BAUMAN: And did you take a school bus to get to and from school then, or how did you—

FLETCHER: Yes. We had—as I said, Art Hackney had a school bus that they owned their own school bus. They had a contract with the district. And there's a picture of myself and my two sisters in that booklet I gave you, waiting for the bus and there's a picture of the bus. It was kind of a—it looks kind of obsolete now, but that was the way they did things then.

BAUMAN: So you graduated high school in 1940.

FLETCHER: 1940. Then I went off to Cheney for a year. And decided I wanted to—didn't want to continue there. I wanted to—I thought I wanted to be an engineer, but I didn't have really the background from the school. At least I could blame it on that. So I transferred to Pullman in my sophomore year. And during beginning of my junior year, I was taken in—I was in the ROTC and we signed up for deferment or whatever you call it, but they said we could finish out the year we were in during my sophomore year. No, it must have been my junior year. That's the third year. But it turned out that they couldn't—they took us, they drafted us and I think it was about January of my junior year in Pullman, from WSU. And at that time I was a member of Sigma Chi. [*laughter*]

BAUMAN: So was that January of 1943 then?

FLETCHER: Yeah, it was.

BAUMAN: At some point that year, of course the federal government started constructing the Hanford Site.

FLETCHER: Right. I came home before—they allowed us, when they called up the ROTC, fellas in Pullman, they gave us a couple weeks to come home and see our folks. So I came home, it must have been the end of January of 1943. And saw my folks, and said goodbye to my sweetheart, Betty Kinsey was her name—became my wife. And after I went back then, I went back to Pullman, and they took us shortly by train from Pullman over to Fort Lewis. And it was an old, real old train that I mention in my booklet that looked like it was one from the pioneer days. There was a—I don't need to go into all the detail, but there was a coal-burning stove in the end of this railway car for heat, and we went over there in the first of February to Fort Lewis. We were not in the army until they took us over there and were forced in it at Fort Lewis. And shortly after that, I got word from my folks that the word had come out that Hanford and White Bluffs and even Richland, it was all going to be taken over by the government for this Hanford project. And that was in, I believe they got word in late February. And the people up at Hanford, which is, of course, is where the actual reactors were, were notified and given about 30 days to evacuate. And my folks, of course, we lived—my dad was the manager of the irrigation district at that time, of the Richland irrigation district. And they had more time because that was where the workers were going to live. But in the meantime they built Camp Hanford out here where we are sitting about right now, and maybe just a little further north. And you probably have the history of Camp Hanford and all that. But anyway, they were allowed to stay I think about six months, whereas the others further up where the reactors were being built, they had to get out quick. And so my folks looked around. They bought a place. My dad, by that time, they offered some of the people work. Most of them were farmers and they wanted to continue farming. And that was my dad. He, by that time, the kids were gone. I was the youngest. The other two, my sisters, were married and off and living on their own. So he decided he'd go back to farming, and they offered him a job to see to some of the irrigation, the way it was continued. But he decided he didn't want to do that. And a number of people did take jobs here for temporary. So where was I now? [*laughter*]

BAUMAN: So your family had six months you said after they were—

FLETCHER: Yeah, about six months. They found a place in Kennewick then, and my dad then bought some place and he put in a fruit orchard over on what became Blossom Hill in Kennewick. And we took over the old house. When I got out of the army—I told you about that in my booklet here, that we took over their house, the two-story house that was on what's now where Denny's is at the corner of Kennewick Avenue and the Umatilla Highway.

BAUMAN: Do you know how much money your parents were given for their—

FLETCHER: In those days, at that time, the government was not as benevolent in their takeover of land. And they did not really offer what the land was worth. So my folks, my dad was one of the leaders of the group that took them to court over the offer. And this lingered on for quite a while, because my dad was one of the—as a manager of the irrigation district. And John Dam that the park is named after, and two or three others, they figured that they were being offered what the land had sold for in Depression days, which had just been more or less begun to get over in 1943. And my folks and others were beginning to feel established, that here they'd worked most of their working lives for 12, 15 years getting to where they felt like they were established and could make a good living. And now they were being offered this, where they had to leave relatively quickly. And not being offered enough to buy something comparable in other areas, where they found they had to pay more than what they had been offered. So this went to court and drug on for a while. They did get a settlement that my dad was involved in. But it took quite a while and it still did not—they were not too happy about it. I'll put it that way. But anyway, they got over it.

BAUMAN: And so you heard about this happening when you were at Fort Lewis?

FLETCHER: Yeah, I was still in the service. I was sent from there to Camp Roberts for infantry training. And I was there until June. See, this happened—I was taken in up in February I guess it was, and we had 13 weeks, almost four months, I think it was, of infantry training there in Camp Roberts in the desert in California. And then I was sent back to New York City. I had an opportunity—then they took some people to specialized training or a specialized training program called ASTP and I was able to get into that because of my college background and I passed some tests, I guess, and so forth. And so I was back there at the time and at Camp Roberts in California at the time that all this took place in Richland, and their dislocation and—

BAUMAN: Do you remember what you thought at the time when you found out?

FLETCHER: [*laughter*] What I thought about that? About all this happening you mean?

BAUMAN: Yeah.

FLETCHER: Well, so much was happening, you didn't have time to think too much about it. Because I was involved in the training and we were kept busy night and day pretty much, and then the infantry training camp and being back there. But I heard about it. They kept me up on it, and there wasn't much you could do about it, and neither could they, because that was it. You could appeal, but that was a long process, the appeal was. So they just took a time to get over it. They got over it eventually.

BAUMAN: Are there any events or things from your childhood growing up in Richland that sort of stand out? Special memories that we haven't talked about yet?

FLETCHER: Probably quite a few things. [*laughter*]

A number of things I mention in his booklet that I gave you. One thing I particularly remember as a kid was I had this pony, and my neighbor kids had ponies too, or else work horses that did the job. And so we could roam around quite a bit. We had a lot of freedom. We all had rifles. We went out hunting. And the jackrabbits were quite numerous, I remember. Going just about a mile from where we are now, there was a sand hill over here off of Stevens Drive, which we called Pole Line Drive. Those days there was a sand

hill over there. And there was an irrigation ditch that ran along this sand
hill. And we'd go in and the boys—take our clothes off and we'd swim in
this irrigation canal. There was a flume there, too, and that was kind of an
interesting thing to go through. And we would take our rifles, and there was
one farm that was close to this sand hill called—I'm trying to remember the
name now, Sam's. Anyway, he had a—his farm was right adjacent to the open
sagebrush land and sand hill. And if you were there in the evening—he had
an alfalfa field right along the edge of this sort of a desert area. At certain
times in the dusk, there'd be whole bunches of jackrabbits would come in.
I remember we would go there with our rifles, and my friends, Dan Barnett
and Richard Hackney and I, and we'd wait for dusk. And you could shoot
these rabbits. And of course Mr. Sandberg I think his name—yeah, Sandberg
was his name, he welcomed anybody that would get rid of the jackrabbits for
him because they were destroying his alfalfa field. And so we'd shoot a bunch
of jackrabbits. And they did have jackrabbit drives once in a while, and they
had pictures of them. I might have some in some of my folks' stuff. But
anyway, we had ponies or horses and we'd go out, and sometimes we'd go up
the river from here, Dan Barnett and Richard Hackney and I. And as I said,
I had a pony that had been caught on the open range and he could outrun
practically any horse around. We would go up there and we'd camp out for
a day and we would find some old prospectors up there. They would be
panning for gold. And I don't think, from the looks of them that they found
very much, but they were interesting characters that'd tell you stories about
their life. And we kind of envied them a little bit, but nobody wanted to do
what they were doing. Anyway, then we would go up there and we'd camp
overnight. Other times, we would go up there—I said that my folks and the
Barnetts and the Hackneys had—we had a boom in the river. We'd catch
driftwood coming down for our—did I tell you about this before?

BAUMAN: No.

FLETCHER: No, okay. If I ramble, tell me. We'd go up, my folks or my dad
and the other men, we would have wagons—we'd hook the work horses to
the wagons. And we'd take enough food to last a couple days. And us boys
would go along, and some other boys were old enough to help, and some
of us were too young to do much, but to tag along and have a good time.
And we'd go up there and we'd set up a camp, and the men would have a log
boom up there. They'd attach logs to each other and run them out into the
water. And when the water would rise in the spring, it would lift these drift
logs from upstream, clear up around where Grand Coulee is now, before

Grand Coulee was built and any other dams. And these drift logs would drift down, if you had a log boom out you'd catch them, as the water would—the high water from the snow melt. And if your log boom was out far enough, you'd get a whole bunch of logs in there and that would be—which then we'd go up and the men would take their team of horses and use their chains to pull these logs out of the water that had been caught in the log boom. And then they'd have to cut them up enough to put on their wagons to haul them down home. And this would take two or three days to do. In the meantime, us kids, the younger ones, we'd have a great time with shooting rabbits and doing some fishing off what was left of the log boom. And fixing our hot dogs over the campfire. It was quite an experience. And we all wanted to go. I think the girls envied us. They couldn't go. I don't remember any of the women going. But when they got the wagons loaded, they had them all—I remember they had sideboards on them, so that they would be loaded up to the maximum. And of course the roads weren't too good. The horses would be really worn out by the time we got these loads down to where we lived. And we'd have to wash them off, rinsing the horses off with a hose because they'd be all that, and it would be quite late in the evening before we made it home. So that was quite a big event in our lives, and especially for the young fellas like us, we thought that was great. I'm sure the men folks were glad it was over. [*laughter*]

BAUMAN: [*laughter*]

FLETCHER: So we had quite a few trips where we went out. I had a friend, Scotty who lived out in Yakima River, and I would go over—he was the one that I think I told you about the time that—maybe it was in my booklet. About the time that our well—the well that we dug up on the top of the hill, the 60 foot well, it had been real cold that winter, and usually the well didn't freeze, but it froze that winter. And so Scotty, my friend, he was the adventurer more so than I was. He said, oh, I can go take a blowtorch down there and thaw it out. Well, he did. My dad let him down this well. The well was hand dug and it was only about so big around. And there were iron steps put in the cement as they went down. As I said, it was 60 feet deep. Of course the water stood up in it about 20 feet or so. It would fluctuate. So Scotty went down with a blowtorch to thaw this pipe out because it had frozen the pump. And he got down there and I guess the confines of the gas or something, it exploded, and he was lucky he wasn't killed. He made it. Somehow it went upward rather than downward and he was able to get out. But his face was black and his eyebrows were singed off. And he was quite a mess from that occasion, but he didn't have to be hospitalized. They put cream on his face and I don't remember whether they got the pipe thawed out or not. I don't think so. I think it took a few days before it got the water up.

BAUMAN: So if someone was to ask you what it was like to grow up in a community like Richland, how would you respond to that? What would you say?

FLETCHER: It was an interesting place to grow up because you were involved in all the activities. You were important as a member of the family. There were chores to do. You also had interesting experiences. You had time to play with your neighbors and develop your own activities and sports to a great extent. I guess probably I look back on it more with rose-colored glasses than it actually was, because I'm sure it was harder for the adults, too. Because it was kind of touch and go for them many times. There was no WPA or relief organizations. People helped their neighbors out when they needed it. I can remember a family that lived not too far from us. The man, the husband died, and they had some fairly young children, the Fraziers. And the wife was left with these—I forgot how young they were—two or three youngsters, and their small farm. And the people of the community just helped out. There was no other organization that they knew of. And later, Bruce Frasier who was in that family, who was about my age. He wasn't a classmate, but he told me years later at the reunions we used to have, he said, did you know— [*emotional*] did you know how much help your mom and dad did—I'm sorry.

BAUMAN: It's all right.

FLETCHER: How much help your mom and dad gave my folks. And I said I had no idea. He told me that my dad and mother, and others—he said it wasn't just them. But they're the ones that made it possible for him to survive. And this, they didn't talk about it at all. Excuse me, cut it off a minute? Wipe my eyes here. I'm glad to get this opportunity. Don't take me wrong.

BAUMAN: That's all right.

FLETCHER: I am glad to get the opportunity to talk. There's not too many people who want to listen to it.

BAUMAN: So I guess is there anything else that we haven't covered that would be important to talk about?

FLETCHER: I think we've covered everything pretty well. I've probably gone side-tracked a lot. And it was a role in that community, as I said, that they did help each other out in many ways. And that they're very independent, too. And there aren't too many of us left. We still get to have a reunion. We did—it's getting down to where there aren't very many of us left. Last year we met at the Old Country Buffet and I had a good time. I think there may have been about 20 of us. But about half of them were descendants, children that brought their parents, who needed help to get there.

BAUMAN: Oh, okay. So this is a reunion of people from Richland?

FLETCHER: The old time Richland, yeah, they lived in old time Richland.

BAUMAN: I just want to thank you very much for coming in today and being willing—

FLETCHER: I enjoyed it.

BAUMAN: —to have me asking questions.

FLETCHER: Okay. I hope that some of it's good use.

BAUMAN: You've been very helpful. Thank you very much.

Leatris Reed, on White Bluffs

*Interview conducted by Robert Bauman, August 27, 2013,
in her home in Walla Walla*

Leatris Reed

BAUMAN: Ready to go? All right. Well, we'll get started. Okay, so let's start first by having you say and spell your name.

REED: My name is Leatris Faye Boehmer Reed. It's pronounced "bay"—"bay-mer." And I was born in North Dakota in 1930. I came here in June to White Bluffs, Washington in 1935 or '36. I'm pretty sure it was '36 because I had my sixth birthday there.

BAUMAN: Why did your family leave North Dakota and head to White Bluffs?

REED: Well, we had a terrible Depression, as you know. And I was a Depression baby, and we just simply weren't—there was no work, there was no money. We just simply had to get out of there. We lost a little boy at two and a half with what they call membranous croup at the time. But it was actually, what it was that awful—oh, kids have it. It's asthma, terrible asthma. And he just couldn't make it. And I think it just broke my mother's heart. She had just lost a baby. So then I became the baby. But I think I was almost six, so—She had written all over Washington, Oregon, because she knew that there was fruit there. And there was food, and the temperature was reasonable. And so she wrote all the little towns that she could find in Washington and Oregon to find out what they did there, what they grew, and what the chances were of people surviving. And she got one from Mr. Reierson that owned the grocery store in White Bluffs, and one from the

149

man who had the bank. And I can't remember his name. But she got glowing letters about the fruit. She got glowing things about that there was work. There was packing sheds, there were alfalfa fields to take care of. And there certainly were. They didn't stint on it and it was not exaggerated.

So that's how we came to be there, and find it we did. It was exactly like they described it. It was probably the best thing that ever happened to us, because we would have starved. We had no money even to pay for that little boy's doctor bill that we left. So then I was the littlest one, and we had six left.

BAUMAN: And so talk a little bit about your parents and your siblings, what your parents' names and your siblings' names—

REED: Well, my oldest sister—who I dearly love and still is alive and I'm glad—is 10 years older than me. And her name is Dorothy Lorraine Boehmer—"bay-mer"—Foyer. And she lives in Everett, Washington, and she will also probably make a statement to you. But she's my oldest. And then I had a sister LaVonne. I had a sister named Helen and a brother named Virgil, all of them the same name, Boehmer. And I had a little brother. I had a sister named Darlene also. And she didn't live at White Bluffs. She stayed with my great-aunt and uncle in Minnesota because they had no children and they wanted to educate her. She was very smart. And she had been treated badly at school in North Dakota, and she didn't want to go back. And they were visiting us. So my mother said, well, you could have her for a year. And of course she—they became so attached to her. And she loved them dearly, and they were good to her. And they did visit us at White Bluffs. And they liked White Bluffs when they came. But it was the best thing that ever happened to us to move to White Bluffs. They had work in packing sheds, like I say. They had—the kids were very receptive to us. And everybody there just opened their arms.

BAUMAN: I wonder if you could describe the place you lived in White Bluffs.

REED: Well, we lived at Lulubelle Johnson's house, and we were buying it from her. But we never realized any money out of when it sold to the government. But Lulubelle Johnson had a son named Ford Johnson because Lulubelle Johnson was a niece of Henry Ford, made the automobiles. And we stayed there at that house and it was just—it was wonderful. We had good neighbors, fruit orchards all over. All over. When they said that you will find all the fruit you want, they really meant it.

BAUMAN: And so what sort of fruit was on the farm you grew up on?

REED: Oh, we had—we grew alfalfa. If you didn't grow alfalfa, you grew fruit. But we had a good well on our land, and alfalfa was a good-paying crop. And of course, we had a cow. And if we had too much alfalfa, we could sell it. So it wasn't something that went bad. And the fruit—every kind of fruit. First time I ever tasted cherries or even seen a cherry tree was there. Or ever ate an apricot or seen an apricot. Or even apples—we had apples there—wonderful. And the whole valley was full of that. It wasn't just one little orchard, it was lots of orchards. It was covered with orchards and alfalfa fields. Yeah.

BAUMAN: Did you have electricity?

REED: We did! First time we had electricity. We had electricity shortly before we moved from North Dakota because I remember my mother had a Maytag washing machine that she had just bought and paid $2 a month for. [*laughter*] So we had that all packed up and ready to go and our tickets—the government gave us tickets to get out of a depressed area. And we took the Empire Builder—brand new—to Spokane, and came into White Bluffs on a fruit train with our little parcel of stuff. And they welcomed us with open arms.

BAUMAN: So you mentioned that there was a well. Is that—how were your crops irrigated with it?

REED: Oh, well, we had sprinkler systems. They weren't like they are now. But what we had, you dug the ditch across the field. And then you made little rows out of that on both sides. And you would run it from the well pipe into that big main ditch. And then you would take the little ditches and close them up. When you've got enough irrigation water, you'd close them back up. And that's what we did. That's how we did it. And that's how they water the orchards.

BAUMAN: And how about running water? Did you have—

REED: We didn't have running water in the house. We went out and got it by the bucketful off of the well. There was a little faucet and you could either pull it up with a bucket or you could turn the faucet on. There was a pump. [*laughter*] It's the same one you watered the yard with. But it was grand to have all the fresh water you needed because we paid $0.25 a barrel in North Dakota for drinking water because it was a rancid and acrid. $0.25 then was a lot of money. We washed clothes with it. My mother would take it after she washed clothes and scrub her floors. And they were white from the lye in the soap. And then she would put it on her garden. But we never had bugs on the garden. [*laughter*] You rationed it really, really carefully there.

BAUMAN: So who were some of your neighbors—

REED: Let me see, Beldins. Beldins were one of our neighbors. Summers were some of our neighbors. And I can't even remember what—his kid's name was—oh, I can't say his name. He kind of talked with a nasal. And my dad called him Snazzy Summers. [*laughter*] I don't know where that came from. But anyways, he was—he had a crush on my sister Helen. And Helen didn't like him. Of course, she was only about 12 or 13. I don't think she had boys in mind. She was kind of a tomboy, too. They were some of our neighbors. And we lived—the Abercrombie place was north of us. And down below us was an abandoned place. And they must have made wine of some kind, because they grew grapes and the grapes were still there. They grew right down to the water. We would go down and get these great big, beautiful Tokay red grapes. And they were right there by the river so they had enough water. But then the whole farm was completely abandoned, probably because of the Depression. I really don't know. But they were the neighboring ones. And the Grewells lived up above us. Helen and Gerald Grewell was their name. And Helen Grewell was my sister Helen's very favorite girl. They'd run around all the time.

BAUMAN: And how about you? Who were some of your best friends—

REED: Oh, Patsy Borden was my best friend for a while. She was probably my best friend, yes. And she was the granddaughter of the Saths, who were related to the Wiehls who run the ferry. And Ida Mae probably was another little friend. She was a nice little girl. I liked them all. We actually—there wasn't a whole lot of—kids had to go home and go do things. It wasn't—I remember the Killian children because they were German. And they came there, I want to say about '37, '38. Hitler was already busy in Germany. And they came home. And they—Mrs. Supple used to raise sheep. Her and husband—they were German also, very, very German. Nice people, but she thought Hitler was doing such great things over there for the German people. And so Mr. Killian went over and had a long talk with her and said, you know, you are putting yourself in a dangerous position, because this is not going well in Germany. He might be doing things for the German people, but he has things in mind for the world. And I thought, how kind. How provocative and kind that was. It wasn't necessary for him to do that. He really didn't know them. But he had heard things. And in a little community, things like that get around. It isn't gossip, it's just fear. But I thought that was very kind. I was only about 7, 8 years old.

BAUMAN: I was going to ask you about—did you have certain chores or responsibilities—

REED: Always.

BAUMAN: —that you had to do on the farm?

REED: Everybody did. Everybody did. Mine was feeding the chickens and gathering the eggs. And we had a little hen named Grandma that mother picked out of the shell, and Billy Rooster, who I guess was named after me. He turned out beautiful. But little Grandma Hen was sterile, so she must have been too weak. But she kept her in the warming oven for an extra couple hours, and she picked her out of the shell. She was sterile. And she would run around stealing everybody else's chicks. She would have a couple of Rhode Island Reds, and she would have a couple of little Leghorns, and maybe a little Barred Rock or two. And she'd huddle them up and boy, she'd fight them off—she's going to keep these kids. Well, Mrs. Sath was such a sweetheart. They lived in the—next to us. And she brought my mother some duck eggs—white Peking duck eggs. And she said, why don't you just set her. She's dying to and she doesn't know—she'd fight them off. And so they set about 10 eggs under her because duck eggs are pretty good sized. And she hatched out every one, and she was so proud of them. Oh, boy, she'd just stomp around that farmyard like she really knew what she was doing. And she just took them down to the horse trough one time. And they found the horse trough, and they jumped in. And she just went berserk—"come back, come back." And so it got to be a morning thing. Every morning she'd take them to the horse trough because they had to have their swim. But she raised them. [*laughter*] Those things were fun things. We didn't have TV. We had a little, tiny radio that we could listen to for the news. But it wasn't a thing you had on all day. But Billy Rooster used to hear the music and he would try to keep up with it. And my sister Dorothy would always do the lunch dishes. She'd say, Billy Rooster, are you out there singing to this music?

BAUMAN: [*laughter*]

REED: It was very wholesome.

BAUMAN: Mm-hm. What other sorts of things did you do for fun?

REED: The river. Oh, the river. The river was a godsend. We learned to swim the first year, the first summer we were there. And we had a raft. The dads had got together and built this big raft. And if you could swim out to the raft—I was not supposed to, but I did. And the little Lowe boy wasn't supposed to, either. He was just learning to swim. And he went under. And my sister Dorothy was a really good swimmer. And he went under for the third time. And she went down and got him, got him out on that—pulled him up. And there was a couple of guys up there pulled him up on that raft and they turned them over on his stomach. And the water just poured. And he lived. But he wouldn't have lived. And every one of those kids at White Bluffs were just as devoted as that to the river. That was our playground. We had to do our work in the morning because it was cool enough. And the summers over there were—boy, they were hot. But we could go in and get in the swimming pool then, our swimming pool.

BAUMAN: You mentioned a little bit ago having a radio. Did you have a telephone also?

REED: We finally did have a telephone. And it was only a dollar a month. That was right uptown. We'd never had one of those before. It was a party line, so if there was an emergency, you had to give up the line. If there was an emergency—if you didn't, they would take your telephone out and you'd never get a telephone again. So that was good and responsible. And I think Mrs. Westling was the telephone—she had it in her home. She and her daughter, I believe, operated it, I'm pretty sure. They lived up by the bank, I remember that. But I can't tell you—we didn't have names on the streets that I know of.

BAUMAN: And so did you get your news mostly on the radio? Was there a newspaper also?

REED: There was. There was a little newspaper there. And I believe it was for Hanford and White Bluffs. And my brother actually worked for that newspaperman. First you start out just because he thought it would be fun. Phil asked him, he said, would you like to know something about publishing a newspaper? And so Dutch went and worked for him. That's what we called him—we didn't call him Virgil. And he went and worked for him. And they did publish a little newspaper. It was a weekly, just once a week. And, of course, they had all the Ladies Aid tea parties, things like that, things at the church. Everything was in there. Yeah, a little gossipy paper. It wasn't malicious. It was just who had a luncheon at their place or whatever. And so, when he got older and came out of the Army, he went and took formal newspapering, went to college and took it. And he became a newspaperman.

Boise Statesman was one of them. And he went down to California. And he worked down there for a while, about 10 years there. So that was good for him.

BAUMAN: He got started in—

REED: Yeah, yeah.

BAUMAN: What businesses do you remember being in White Bluffs?

REED: Well, I remember Reierson's Grocery. And I remember around the back of it was a little creamery where you could—in fact, they picked up a can of cream at our back porch every morning, because we had, by then, two cows. And one was a Guernsey and one was a Jersey, and they both had lots of cream. So we couldn't use all the cream, even for six kids. [*laughter*] So they would come and pick that up. And my sister, Helen, always did the ironing. She liked to iron. That was her job. And so he would come, and here she'd be on that back porch, early in the morning, starting the ironing. [*laughter*] And he says, I don't think you've gone to bed. He was a kidder. But that was what she did, and she was excellent at it.

BAUMAN: So there was Reierson's and—

REED: And the creamery. And there was a little garage back there, and I can't remember the name of it because we didn't have a car. But there was a little garage back there. And there was Pop English's drugstore. Everybody knew where that was. Pop English and his wife had no children. But they owned this little drugstore. And they made the best ice cream in the world, and he sold it there. And you could have an ice cream cone for a nickel. I mean it was an ice cream cone. And a dime was a double dipper, and it had two shelves and then one cone—it went down to one cone. And that was a dime. And it was hard, if you had a dime, to decide whether you wanted to do that or not. I remember my mother used to give us two pennies for Jesus to take to Sunday school. And I always put one in. I figured Jesus wouldn't care if I have a rope licorice from Pop English's. And years later, I told her, I said, Mama, if I would have known that Jesus didn't want my money like I do now—he wants our love, has nothing to do with my two cents—I would have brought you home one. She says, your Sunday school dress was the messiest thing ever. She says it was always was covered in black. And, she says, the rest of the girls I could just press the back of that little white dress with some water and make it good for next Sunday. And she says, they could wear a Sunday school dress for all month, but not you. [*laughter*]

BAUMAN: Oh, talking about the school in White Bluffs, how large was it, how many students do you think there were, and maybe the teachers that you remember particularly—

REED: I would say that, in my first and second grade class, there was 18 that I can name off, that I can remember. We had a little boy come there named Carter House. And I think his father was something to do with engineering. Allard, Sam Allard kept the irrigation system and the electric thing, and I think Mr. House had something to do with it. But we had never seen a child look like this before. He looked like he stepped out of a catalog. He had this blonde—beautiful boy—had this little blonde hair all cut so nice. And he wore little argyle knee socks and little suit pants and a little white shirt and little slaps on his shoes. And I thought, my gosh, that's the cutest little boy I've ever seen. And, of course, he didn't know how to share. And one day I was swinging on the swing, and Alice Moody looked out the window. And here was this little boy grabbing that swing and taking it away from me. And she says, we don't do that here. She says, you have to wait your turn. She says, when Leatris is done with it, she says, you can have it. It'll be your turn. [*laughter*] But they were probably nice people, it's just that they weren't White Bluffs-oriented.

BAUMAN: And so you want to talk about Alice Moody a little bit? She was your first—

REED: Ah, she was a wonderful teacher.

BAUMAN: —grade teacher, is that right?

REED: Wonderful lady. She taught first, second, and, I believe, possibly third. And there was probably, I would suppose, 18 in the first grade, and probably close to that in second. And then there was the third grade. And we had— we did not have separate rooms, but we had little partitions that she would put up so that we would keep our attention. And we did have monitors. Everybody helped everybody. If there was a little boy that needed help with numbers and somebody was good with it, she would assign them to help that child. It wasn't—it was probably the most together community. If something was unfair on the playground, it was put a stop to right away, sometimes by the children. And teachers, if they were in their room, they kept a window open in good weather because if there was anything wrong in the playground, it was either reported or taken care of. And I can't remember fights on school. I can't remember that, ever. It would never have been tolerated.

BAUMAN: How did you get to school, did you walk—

REED: Oh, yes.

BAUMAN: —or did you ride the bus?

REED: Everybody walked. The only children I remember that came in on a bus—oh, what was his name—Mr. Fisher's school bus. Mr. Fisher, I believe. And he came in on a little bus—with a little bus. And I think they were probably from out toward Saddle Mountain and farms like that because they had to go to school. But I do remember a little bus. And I don't even remember that it was painted yellow or anything. I think it kind of reminded me of maybe a van. But it had windows in it and it was kind of squared. It seems like it was dark gray.

BAUMAN: Mm-hm. And so how far was the school from your home?

REED: Oh, I, let me see. We had to pass Saths' orchard, the whole length of their orchard, and then Beldins'. And then we had to walk across the front of Beldins' and it was pretty good sized. And then we had to walk up past Summers' up the hill to our house. So I would suppose it was probably a mile. And some of them walked a lot more than that. And Mrs. Moody used to bring kids in with her when she came to school because she drove to school. And she was around the Reach, around the—it was last reactor. And Old Town used to be there. The whole town used to be on the river at one time. But they moved it away because I think they were progressing. People were moving in, spreading out. Orchards were filling in. And I think that's why they probably moved the town. But we had a movie theater. We had a movie theater. And somebody from the Tri-Cities came over with a movie. In the summertime, we had a movie once a week, probably in the evening early, about seven. And then, in the wintertime, it was kind of hit and miss whenever they could get over or whatever, I don't know. I can't remember. But we did have movies there.

BAUMAN: Do you remember any movies that you saw over there?

REED: No, I wouldn't remember that. I probably wouldn't even have understood it. But it wasn't anything that was offensive because they didn't do that.

BAUMAN: Where was the movie theater in relationship to some of the other businesses—

REED: Okay, across the street from Reierson's Grocery, and also across the cross street where the railroad came to fill the cars, that was right across the street from Reierson's Grocery as you come in to White Bluffs. Then there was a main drag. And there was a railroad hotel there, because they had railroad workers that, when they went out to do things to the railroad— the rails out there—they had to have people. And then they also rented to other people if they came in and there was a room empty. And it was right across the street from Reierson's Grocery from this one that's burned off. And behind there was a building. And that's where they had the movie theater. And it was just an old building, I don't know. It had seats in it—not wonderful, but seats. And then they had a balcony on it, too, so that was good. Kids would go up there and of course, you know. One time we had some holy rollers in there that rented it. [*laughter*] And they were rolling around on the floor. And my brother and his buddies were up there taking toilet paper, throwing rolls down there. They were all in little—I don't know, rolling around. [*laughter*] The Spirit moved them, I guess. Boy, they got in trouble for that. [*laughter*] But it was used for a lot of things. If they had a community meeting or something, they'd either use it, the high school or that little building, depending on what it was about. Sometimes it was a farm meeting, or a new spray that was coming out, or what they should do and shouldn't do.

BAUMAN: Mm-hm. I was going to ask you about any community events that you remember, either picnics, or Fourth of July things, or boat races—

REED: Boat races we had right there. They did not start in Tri-Cities. They started at White Bluffs. It was wonderful. Mr. Killian used to slice his big watermelons and sell them for $0.05. [*laughter*] Pop English used to sell his ice cream cones. Oh, and the Ladies Aid always had something going— cookies or something or a bake sale. And it was just a fun time. And we had a band. We used to gather up a band and have music there. It was pretty good. And in the spring, we always had a little May Day thing. And we had a maypole. And they would twine the strings around it like they do. And we had a program—quite a program—at the high school. And we had one that we were in that was the doll dance. And Alice Beyers was supposed to be the French lady who had the dolls. And so we had these cute little dresses on, little ballerina-type dresses. And she would come around and wind us up. That was the first start of it, and we danced to the tune, the doll dance. And each one of us she wound up. And we started dancing. And we would dance around this maypole. And that was part of the program. And we had—oh, I remember my sister had a reading. "I want to live in the house by the side of the road, and be a friend of man," is the way it goes. And each stanza ends with that. And every single—my mother tutored her, her teacher tutored her—and at the end of every one of those stanzas when she got up there, "I want to live in the house by the side of the road and be friendly with men." It brought down the house, of course. Oh, my mother was so embarrassed. She was so embarrassed. [*laughter*] So when she—later in life—when she had a beautiful garden and a family of her own, I found that on a plaque that you put out in your garden, an open book with this on it in a plaque form. And it said, "I want to live in the house by the side of the road and be a friend to man." [*laughter*] I said, this is for old memories, Helen, and she laughed. She had a good laugh out of that.

BAUMAN: You mentioned earlier your Sunday school dress. What church did you go to?

REED: Well, I think at that—first, we went to the Presbyterian, but then they closed that. But then we went to the little Lutheran church I think was up in back of the bank. And we went there for a while. But my dress was always a mess. I come home with licorice all over it because, of course, I had to stop and take one of those pennies, buy a licorice at Pop English's drugstore.

BAUMAN: Do you remember any other churches in the community?

REED: I do not. I don't remember that there was Catholic church there. I don't remember that there was.

BAUMAN: I wonder—I know that the Wanapum people were in the area. I wonder if you have any memories of the Wanapum Indians, or—

REED: Oh, yes. We had—I don't know that they—they were Johnny Buck's Indian tribe. My brother knew Frank Buck. He had two wives. One was old and had white hair, and her name was Deloria. And I don't remember the other one. But they were fine people. They came in and they would gather fruit off the ground because it was ready to dry. They would catch fish out of that river and smoke it and just grab your nose and want you to go down there and have some. And they were just fine people. They came in usually before cherries—you would see them before cherries—and then you would see them every day out in the orchards. And nobody ever charged anybody for that. They could have all they wanted. And my mother actually learned to dry fruit. And oh, that smelled good, just waft up and grab you by the nose. And they put it in little, thin sheets like cheesecloth. They'd make a rack with willows—make a rack, weave it, and put it between maybe stumps of willows, little tiny seedling willows that were coming up. And they would make these racks. And they would put this cheesecloth over it to keep the flies away. And they would dry it. And they would dry fruit all summer long—peaches, cherries, apricot, apples, everything. And they taught my mother that if you soak them just a few minutes in saltwater, they will not turn brown. And they won't salt the fruit. And so she learned how to do that. And the fish—oh! When they smoked that fish, you wanted to go down there and just have some. It just smelled delicious. They had a mixture they mixed up to put on it so it wouldn't dry it out. And they would take the whole bone out of it. They'd slice it. They take the scale off, the skin off, and the ribs out. And they would place that between these same little cloths and dry it. And they would smoke it from beneath and they'd keep that just really low. Oh, you could smell it all over the valley. You'd just—oh! And it was delicious. They did a good job. And they were interesting. Interesting, interesting people. I remember my brother used go up, 14 or 15 years old, he and his two buddies Leo and Louie Russo—Leo Goodner and Louie Russo—and they'd go up to Saddle Mountain, take a little flour and little baking powder and maybe some salt and some lard. And they'd go up there and stay for a couple days. Nobody thought anything of it. There was a little spring up there and it was always green. And they'd just camp out and snare a rabbit or whatever. They just couldn't—they just loved it. Usually he went in good weather, yes. But we didn't have bad weather in summertime. But you wouldn't let a 14-year-old kid out now, three of them all by themselves? [*laughter*] But they had wonderful times. And it was a good place to raise kids, and it was good place to be raised, too. Really good.

BAUMAN: I want to ask you about the sheriff.

REED: Oh, Roy Bean was a fine man. I think I told you about him coming to get the boys to take the—

BAUMAN: You did before we started recording on the film—

REED: Well, he was a deputy sheriff out of the Tri-Cities. And I think the main thing—the office was up in probably Yakima, I'm not sure. But he had two little girls. And Roberta went to school with me. And Loretta came along later. She was younger by a couple of years. But he came to our house one morning, and he—we were just up. Dutch wasn't up yet, my brother. But he said, I wonder, is Virgil up yet? And he said, no, he said, but I'll go get him. He said, what's he done now? And he says, he's sure going to get it if he's gotten into trouble. And he says, now I want you to understand. He says, there's nothing going to be trouble about this, Joe. He says, I want you to go get him up. He says, his two buddies are in my car. And, he says, we're going to do a little favor for some people. And he said, I don't want any repercussions about this. I don't want any questions about it. If I hear of any beatings about this, he says, I will deal with it. And my dad went in and got Dutch up. And he came out and got in the car. He was dressed. And they went up to the packing house, which is right across from Reierson's Grocery. And he says, now, we're going to go get that car, which you pushed down this incline last night and released the brake. And he says, we're going to push it back up that slight hill. It was probably down there about seven, eight blocks. Well, it was uphill, now. It wasn't so easy. But, he says, I'll help you with the brake here. And he said, we'll keep this released. And he said, we'll push this back up. So he got those three boys—probably 14, 15 years old—to push that car about seven or eight blocks up to be iced. And he came home. He was pretty sweaty and he was pretty tired. And he wanted some breakfast. [*laughter*] But nothing was ever mentioned about it. And he was a fine man. He knew how to handle people. And he wasn't out there to bully anybody or—and later, he came to a family reunion. We called him up and invited him, because we knew he'd lived in Milton-Freewater, him and his wife. And, of course, Roberta—I kept track of Roberta because she moved here. That was his oldest daughter. And so I was glad to meet them. And we invited him to the get-together. And he mentioned that. And he laughed about it to Dutch. Dutch was a little uneasy when he thought we were going to invite the Beans. [*laughter*] And I said, he made a good joke out of it. He says, I've used that a lot of times, he said, on how to and how not to. And he said, you turned out pretty good. He says, turned out pretty good.

BAUMAN: Someone else I wanted to ask you about—when we were talking earlier, you were mentioning a man named Ellis John—

REED: Oh, Ellis John was an interesting person. He lived down in old town in just one of the abandoned buildings. He had been on some kind of a merchant ship. And somebody on that ship that worked with him attacked him. And he was beating on him, and he killed him. And so they sent him to a penitentiary. It was a kind of an accidental killing. He didn't mean to but he was really—that's what I got out of it. But he lived there. He came to White Bluffs because it was such a nice little town. He came through there and he liked it. And he was an artist, a real artist. He did pictures of people. And he would make a few bucks, did paintings of them. And when I had my

10th birthday—my mother used to leave vegetables and fruit on his porch because she knew he didn't have a garden. And she always left vegetables and fruit if we had extra—because we always had extra—on his porch because he was kind of a recluse. But he would come out and talk to you. He was pleasant. And when I had my 10th birthday, my folks bought Muriel Beldin's girl's bike for me to ride. And it was a smaller bike. And he painted roses on the fenders of that blue and white bike. And I had the prettiest bike in town when I moved to Walla Walla. [*laughter*] So I always remembered him because I was fascinated with—in fact, I took art in school because I was so fascinated with him. He would sit there and sketch somebody and—right in front of your eyes—and make it live. And you wondered how he did that. He used charcoal a lot, and pen and ink, and paint. Just—and I always felt bad because his life was kind of wasted there. He could've been—I mean he could make a likeness of anybody perfectly. But he chose to be there because we accepted him, and we respected his privacy. He had been through a lot. And I don't think he was a murderous person. I think it was something that happened.

BAUMAN: So when and why did your family leave White Bluffs?

REED: Well, in 1937, Hitler was very busy. And by 1941, he was even busier. And in June—in April of 1941, we moved to Walla Walla. My dad says, there's going to be some military. He says, you can bet your sweet life. He says, it's big enough to have some military. And he said, I want to be where there's some jobs. And so we moved to Walla Walla. And there was a veterans' hospital here and he was a veteran. And he said, I just think it'd be better, because they had surveyed our area in 1937, '36 or '37, I'm not sure which. But we kept surveyors at our house, so we knew they were surveying for something. And it took them, oh, a couple years to survey all that area that they were looking at.

BAUMAN: But you didn't know what they were—

REED: They didn't even know what they were surveying for. They were hired by the United States government. And they were employees of the United States government. So we kept Mama and Daddy Redd, we called them. And they were nice people. They had no children, and they just loved us. They just—she taught us really good things, things that we hadn't learned from our mom. Mama didn't know how to make fudge. She'd never had that much sugar to spare in her life. [*laughter*] So we all learned how to make fudge and penuche and good stuff from Ma Redd.

BAUMAN: So you knew they were working for the government, but you didn't know—

REED: We didn't know. They didn't know. But they were there about, I would say, two years. So I associate it with the Manhattan Project because it's a logical. Hitler was busy. Oh boy, was he busy. So I don't know. It might have been, it might not have been. We thought it was an irrigation project. We were so excited, because an irrigation project would have given us more, see, I mean, you could have irrigated more land. But—

BAUMAN: So how old were you when you left White Bluffs and you moved—

REED: I had my 11th birthday here. It was in the spring of 1941. And we didn't have war until 1941, December 7.

BAUMAN: So as a 10- and 11-year-old girl, what did you think of leaving White Bluffs and moving to Walla Walla?

REED: Oh, I thought I was going to die. For one thing, they had a Holstein cow over at Margaret Stearns's where we lived in her little house when we came here. And my father took care of her yard and milked her cow and separated the milk. It was a Holstein cow. That's like skim milk. I didn't drink milk for a year. I couldn't handle it. I mean, we were used to—we had cream on top of the milk. And then we sold half of it to the little dairy. And, I says, this is what we slop the pigs with. I'm not drinking this. And they worried about me—I wasn't drinking milk. But it was probably better for me, but I wasn't used to it. I wasn't used to it. The Scandinavian blood in me calls for that milk with the fat in it. [laughter]

BAUMAN: Did you keep in contact with the people from White Bluffs after you moved here to Walla Walla?

REED: I knew Bonnie Morris was here, and her sister, Ruth—her sister-in-law, Ruth. They were both Morris girls. And I don't think they were sisters. I think they were cousins because we had two Morris families there. But Ruth went to school with my sister Dorothy at White Bluffs High School. And I went to school with Bonnie Morris, who went to White Bluffs Grade School. And I'll tell you what, I was sure jealous of that girl. She could do handstands and cartwheels all around the White Bluffs Grade School and not stop. She could do a flip over and throw herself up and come down on her feet. And I just—I was just amazed. She was a couple years older than me, or I thought she was. But I don't think so. I think she was probably close to my age. She probably—maybe it was one year. But she was a fantastic athlete. Even the boys envied her. I mean, she could just flip around like a circus performer. And here I was, a tomboy, but not delightful with things like gymnastics. There was always somebody we envy when we were kids.

BAUMAN: So in 1943, a couple years after you moved away, the federal government came in and—

REED: Cleaned out everything.

BAUMAN: —everybody had to leave. Did you hear about that from people you used—

REED: My sister was living there.

BAUMAN: Oh, she was, okay.

REED: She was living in the Johnson place. She said nobody ever came and got the beautiful antiques she had upstairs. She had a teapot that came over on the Mayflower. The legs were—it was a silver teapot, and the legs were actually worn completely off. And it had the Ford name on it.

BAUMAN: So which sister was this, then, who had—

REED: That was Dorothy, my oldest sister that I love so much.

BAUMAN: And why had she stayed there?

REED: She stayed there because she had a husband who was a truck driver. And she was expecting her first baby and didn't really know what else to do. And he was gone.

BAUMAN: Was this someone she had met in White Bluffs, then, or—

REED: She met him in Kennewick. She was working at Kennewick General Hospital at the time. And she met Vern Fouracre. And they got married at our house. In fact, we chivareed them at our house. And that was probably when—I was 13 when I was an aunt, so Colleen was born in '43. And she wasn't born there. She was born—she was pregnant when she was there but she was born after that. And that's when they moved them out. They had to move everybody out. And I always wondered whatever became of Mrs. Johnson's beautiful things, because they were museum things. They should've been in a museum. They shouldn't have been in an attic.

BAUMAN: Right. Where did your sister and her husband go, then, when they had to leave?

REED: Well, they went back to Kennewick. And Colleen was born in Kennewick. Then she came to Walla Walla. And she had a little boy a year or two later. She had four.

BAUMAN: Have you ever gone back to—

REED: We went to the Hanford-White Bluffs picnics, I think, four or five times. And then, of course, the people who were doing the arranging for it—Annette Heriford and I can't remember the other boy. I can't remember the boy.

MAN OFF-CAMERA: Bob Grisham, maybe?

REED: I believe, I believe. They graduated high school with Dorothy. And they just were getting too old to do that. And it was hard thing. And people were dying off. But Alice Moody was at the last one. I was, too. And I loved seeing her. And I knew her immediately. She looked just like herself, just exactly.

BAUMAN: So when you went to the reunions, it usually was a picnic, right, at the park, Howard Amon Park. Did you also do a tour—

REED: Mm-hm. We did, we did. We could take our car in. First time, I think they had a bus for people who had no transportation, because the Tri-Cities had—they were old. Some people weren't driving anymore. So they evidently had acquired a bus for some that couldn't. And whoever had room in cars, we took them. But ours was always full because our kids were just fascinated by this. And we went to the dinners, little banquets that we had you. Mr. Reierson was there.

BAUMAN: What did you think when you had a chance to go back and see the land, the area where—

REED: Broke my heart. Just broke my heart. We had a hard time finding—we wouldn't have found where our house was, except there was a water tank associated with this pump. And it set out front. It was made—and a lot of the people had them. Some of them had brick with a liner in it. But this one was cement and was kind of cone-shaped, and evidently was a holding tank for the house, or whatever. I don't know, I'm not sure. But it was there. And that was still there. They hadn't knocked that down. That's the only way—and it set up on a hill. It was the first row of hills as you came down toward the river—dropped down the river to Old Town. And so, that was how we found it. But there wasn't any stumps of trees left. There wasn't anything left. They actually had the crew of conscientious objectors at McNeil Island come down and cut the trees and the wood out of there, and took it back for fuel by truckloads. And that was the last, just before they released—they were already starting to build the reactors and things and dig the systems underneath, and storage thing under the—But it was a wonderful place to grow up, and I don't know that they'll ever get it cleaned up.

BAUMAN: Anything that we haven't talked about yet in terms of White Bluffs, any stories or events that stand out that we haven't had a chance to talk about?

REED: I just think it was the best place to the world to raise kids because there was a community spirit—that I never saw favoritism. I never saw belligerence about minding rules. I always saw a humanitarianism. If you knew that your husband or your neighbors or anybody was having a problem, you didn't make it your business. You didn't gossip about it. It wasn't a usual. It was more of any empathy, more of a sympathetic, let's just do what we can for them. I never saw the malice toward anybody because they were poor or maybe did something wrong. If there was a wrong committed, it was straightened out and talked about by the two people that did it. And it was left alone. And they had a tavern there. [AUDIO OUT] And, even there, it was not tolerated for people to act like a bunch of savages or fights or—It was a place to go have a cold beer if you wanted one, but I don't remember a lot of drunkenness or—I don't think he would have—Harry somebody was his name. It ended up two people owned it, but I can't remember what their name was.

BAUMAN: Oh, the tavern?

REED: And we were gone, but they told us about it. And I can't remember, but that was the last of it. And it was just a little tavern. I probably, I don't know—it was probably four or five little tables and maybe a row along the bar. I remember standing out there one time because my dad went in to have a beer with a friend. And I said, well I'll wait out here and eat this ice cream cone from Pop English. [*laughter*] I knew what to do with it. He was a fine man. He actually organized the White Bluffs band.

BAUMAN: Oh, right.

REED: The high school band. And he made room for everybody. Everybody had—Ola Meeks could do the baton twirl, and she taught two other girls to do that. And they had white pants with a—it's either black or navy blue stripe down the side—and a white shirt, just a plain little white shirt. The girls wore a white blouse. And everybody had a part in high school band. And they went up to Yakima and they took first place. That little—and competing against Kennewick, Pasco? It was amazing! Somewhere we have a picture, and I don't have the picture. I can't find it. [*laughter*] But Dorothy just loved it. She played a drum, and she just loved it. And they did a good job. No, it was a fine place to grow up. And it was sad, because it really was a neighborhood community. And there were people who had plenty, I mean, they had—there were well-to-do people there. But they didn't flaunt it. They were no different when they went to the Grange meeting. Or whether they were entertaining, it was not—there was not any class distinction. And especially at school I noticed it. That's unusual. That's unusual. And we welcomed it.

BAUMAN: Well, I want to thank you very much for letting us come here and talk to you today, and for sharing your memories—

REED: Well, you use what you can. I know you you'll cut, because, of course, you can't. You have to do what you have to do. But I know that people are going to give you some wonderful stories, stories about how they were accepted. And I'm sure every one of those people that you interview will tell you the same thing, that it was a wonderful community.

BAUMAN: Thanks again very much. I appreciate it.

REED: I appreciate your coming.

Dick Wiehl, on White Bluffs

Interview conducted by Robert Bauman, June 25, 2013,
campus of Washington State University Tri-Cities

Dick Wiehl

BAUMAN: In this oral history interview with Dick Wiehl, I'll be talking to Mr. Wiehl about his family's history, particularly their history in White Bluffs and the area around there. So I'm going to start with maybe talking about your family first, asking about them. Do you know how and when they came to the White Bluffs area?

DICK WIEHL: Well, my grandfather—that's who we're talking about—came in the late 1890s, and it was as a result of advertisement, which was nationwide, I suppose, at the time to get people out here to populate the area. And he came out with the prospect of buying some acreage, which he did, and upon which they established a ranch. And that would have been in the very latest part of the 1890s.

BAUMAN: And do you know where he came from?

WIEHL: Minnesota.

BAUMAN: Did he come by himself?

WIEHL: He came with his father, initially. Then his father went back and lived the rest of his life back in Minnesota. He had a good position back there, but this was an opportunity for a young man to strike out on his own and see if the road was, indeed, paved with gold in the West. And that's how the land was sold.

BAUMAN: Sure. Do you know much about your mother's family? I'm sorry, your grandmother's family, the Craig family, right?

WIEHL: Yeah, and she was Hattie Wright from the Craig family. And she came from Ellensburg, so she was out here even before my grandfather. And how they met, I don't know. But I do know that they were married about 1900, and then moved on together and onto the ranch that my grandfather was then establishing on the banks of the Columbia River.

BAUMAN: So could you describe the ranch? I know you didn't really live there, but you spent some summers there.

WIEHL: Well, I was born in 1936, and they were out of there in 1943. So those were the years that—obviously, I don't remember much from 1936. But from about 1940 on, I do. I have vivid memories and stories that were told. And so that's really where my relationship started was about that time.

BAUMAN: Can you describe the ranch?

WIEHL: It was, in my perspective, it was huge. [*laughter*] And it was. There were thousands of acres that were leased, and the ranch, kind of the official ranch itself, was several hundred acres. And, of course, to a child at that time, I'd go with my grandfather, and we'd go horseback riding, and he would be checking on various operations on the ranch on a day-to-day basis, and we'd go all day. [*laughter*] And have lunch somewhere in saddle bags, and then come back by evening. And we'd be gone from 7 o'clock in the morning until 6 o'clock in the evening, just riding on the ranch. Never left it. So it was a big ranch.

BAUMAN: Right. So what sort of crops did your grandfather grow?

WIEHL: Well, the crops I remember specifically, because I was out there picking potato bugs, were the potatoes. And so they grew potatoes. They had gardens. They were completely self-sufficient. And I remember my grandmother out there working in a large garden, and the other vegetables that they had I wouldn't recall. But there were lots of them, and the potatoes were where I would come in. And they had cattle, a lot of cattle, which were on the rangeland that they had leased. They had goats. They had chickens. And just had horses, obviously horses. Just about every animal that you would need in an operating ranch. And some of the animals were work animals, and some of them were riding, some of the horses were riding horses. And they had a lot of them. And just the care and maintenance of those animals was a full-time job, which was generally done by the women— meaning my grandmother, or the younger kids when they were there, or then eventually my aunt, who was a teenager when they had to move out of there in 1943. Just took care of the chickens and things like that.

BAUMAN: Now did you have siblings or cousins who would spend the summer there?

WIEHL: No. I had a younger sister, but she was too young to be involved in that.

BAUMAN: And now the cattle, did they sell any of the cattle?

WIEHL: Oh, yeah. They were involved in the cattle markets, and I can remember the wailing and moaning over the, this is a Republican cattle market, or this is a Democratic cattle market. [*laughter*] Whether things were up or down, that's the way they would talk about it. And they could always blame somebody for the fact that the market was down. So that was important to them.

BAUMAN: Do you have any idea where they sold the cattle?

WIEHL: No, no, no.

BAUMAN: So what other buildings were there besides the ranch house itself?

WIEHL: The main ranch house, and then there were a cold room, a big refrigerator, actually, which was an ice room. Several buildings, which were— The house fronted on a lane. The lane was the highway that actually ran through from Othello and Moses Lake to the Columbia River, where you'd catch it to go over to White Bluffs, which was immediately across the river. And so their front yard was immediately contiguous to that road. Across the road were several buildings. I don't recall how many, but several for machinery. Barns, lean-tos, rather ramshackle but utilitarian structures for the housing machinery. And then they had chicken coops, and they raised goats, and they had goat houses, and so they had a lot of outlying buildings, which were particularized for a certain function on the ranch.

BAUMAN: And when you spent summers there, was there, for instance, electricity?

WIEHL: No. There was a telephone, and that was—When I was originally there, there wasn't electricity. In fact, I don't know if there ever was electricity. I think that it was coming, and it may have been there in the latter years, but that was relatively new, if there at all. The telephone, I do remember, because that was exciting when anybody on the line got a call, because everybody was included in it. [*laughter*] You'd dial an operator, a central operator that was in White Bluffs. I'm sure that must've been where she was. And she was on a first name basis with everybody. It was one ring here and two rings there, and so the telephone was quite an active source of getting the word out in the small community.

BAUMAN: So how'd that work? So if the phone rang in the house—

WIEHL: It'd be two rings; that meant it was your phone.

BAUMAN: If it was more than that—

WIEHL: Or less, it was somebody else's phone. It didn't make any difference. Everybody went over and got it. [*laughter*] And sometimes they'd even join into the conversation when they weren't supposed to be even on the line.

BAUMAN: Not a whole lot of privacy.

WIEHL: No.

BAUMAN: [*laughter*] And then what about irrigation? You must have had some sort of irrigation?

WIEHL: They had irrigation. I can remember wandering through the fields with my grandfather as he—There was blockages that occurred from time to time in the ditches that were coming out from the—there were outlets for the water. And they had a good irrigation system. They must have taken the water right out of the Columbia, pumped it up there, and distributed it, because the ranch was on a level, probably two or three feet above the Columbia River. So it wouldn't have been difficult to do. Lots of pipe. I remember he had a shipment of pipe come in one time when I was there.

BAUMAN: What kind of pipe? Like cement?

WIEHL: Yeah. It was, and it was very, very heavy. It'd last forever, I thought, not realizing that the government was going to probably dig it all up in a couple of years.

BAUMAN: Right. And then what about the house itself? Do you remember how large it was, how many bedrooms, or anything like that?

WIEHL: It had two bedrooms, a master bedroom and a kid's bedroom, because when I was there, my aunt was still—she was just a couple years older than I. And so she had her bedroom, and my grandparents had their bedroom, and then there was a large sleeping porch on one end of the house, where since I was there in the summertime, I would sleep with my grandfather on this sleeping porch. And there were a room for a couple of other people to sleep out there too if we had guests or something like that. And then there was a huge room in the center of the house, where they had community gatherings. I mean, it was that big. So that if the local farmers wanted to get together for a meeting of some kind followed by snacks or even a dance, they would always have it in that what Grandpa called the great hall. And it was large by my estimation. And then they had the other big room in the center of the house was the kitchen and dining area. And those are the rooms I remember. I'm sure there probably were other rooms that I was never even shown to. But those are the rooms I remember.

BAUMAN: So it was a place where people came.

WIEHL: Oh, yes, oh, yes.

BAUMAN: Yeah.

WIEHL: Very definitely.

BAUMAN: Wow. And at the time you were there, it was a larger house that had that?

WIEHL: Yes. They kept adding on until—I think it probably took its final shape in about 1920.

BAUMAN: Wow. Now, you mentioned your aunt. I wonder if you could just for clarification, state the children, or I guess in your father's generation, who—

WIEHL: Well, all right. My dad was born in 1909. Wright, the oldest, was born in 1903. And Elroy, the youngest boy, was, I would say, 1920. And my aunt was 1933.

BAUMAN: Okay.

WIEHL: Quite a range. [*laughter*]

BAUMAN: Yeah. About 20 years.

WIEHL: Yeah. For that time, it was quite a range.

BAUMAN: And you were born?

WIEHL: In 1936.

BAUMAN: 1936. In Yakima?

WIEHL: In Yakima, yeah.

BAUMAN: And so your family was in Yakima—

WIEHL: Yes.

BAUMAN: But you would spend summers—

WIEHL: Yes, I couldn't wait for the summers. I had to get over there and spend time with—Well, I was the baby at that point, and so I loved that. And loved to get over there and play with his tractors. And that's what I would do. He had several tractors. The one that I liked was a very nice John Deere big green tractor. But it was a small tractor for those times. And so I could actually sit on the seat, and by the time I was six, I could reach the pedals. Now to guard against anything ever happening, the battery was always taken out when I came over there, so nothing would go awry. [*laughter*] One time I came over though, and I think it was either in '41 or '42, because I had to be at least that old. We pulled down into the driveway, and I jumped out of the car and ran over to the tractor, which was sitting out on the road. I mean, this was the highway that it was sitting out on, which, as I explained earlier, just kind of ran right through the property. And I didn't know it, but the tractor had been used that morning, and my grandpa didn't know exactly when we were coming. In any event, he didn't take the battery out of the tractor. So I jumped on and did what I'd always hoped I could do: drive the tractor. It started, and everybody was standing back completely amazed and shocked and dazed, because I roared down the street. [*laughter*] And Dad was running after me and Grandfather on the other side. And I basically said, it's under control. Went down about 100 yards, turned around, brought the tractor back, and stopped it. And Grandpa said, well, I guess we don't have to take the battery out anymore. [*laughter*] But thinking of that, what really kind of alarmed me was the fact that I was driving the tractor and having things under perfect control, I thought. But I was a little concerned about my dad running alongside on one side and my grandfather on the other. I didn't think they could hold up a lot longer.

BAUMAN: [*laughter*] That's a great memory.

WIEHL: Yeah.

BAUMAN: So when you were there in the summers, you picked a lot of potato bugs, and you would ride out with your grandfather?

WIEHL: Right. And just a lot of times sometimes play with my aunt. We would go exploring, and the property was vast, and there was always something, a place to go, an island to visit, and so we would just do what kids do, and swim in the Columbia River, and she raised a lot of little chickens.

And so we would go out and count the chickens and make sure they were fed and play with them. They were very cute little things. And games. I mean, it was a time when kids would play board games. And so we got pretty good at a couple of those.

BAUMAN: And you mentioned it was right on sort of the main road.

WIEHL: Right. It went right through the ranch.

BAUMAN: Right. So were there a lot of people driving through?

WIEHL: From time to time. Nothing like today. But no, there would be two or three cars that I would see a day going in both directions. And I don't even know whether they had a ferry schedule, but I know that my grandfather would go down there at a certain time, which was a horse ride, it would have probably been about a three-minute horse ride down to where the ferry was. And so he was committed to be there at certain hours. So from that, I assume there must've been some sort of schedule, but he wasn't there on call.

BAUMAN: So he would, was operating the ferry, take the ferry—

WIEHL: Back and forth.

BAUMAN: Back and forth to the car on the other side.

WIEHL: Yeah. And the whole procedure wouldn't take very long after he got the ferry started up.

BAUMAN: So was he—

WIEHL: And I went down with him a lot of times. And that was a big thrill, because he would, if they were old diesel, it was an old diesel engine, and he would get that. It seemed like it took forever to get that fired up, but when it was, it would go clunk, de-clunk, de-clunk, de-clunk, and then we would go, de-clunk, de-clunk, de-clunk across the load one place or the other. I don't remember, but it was back and forth. And if there were—

BAUMAN: How long did it take?

WIEHL: Oh, the ferry ride itself, maybe five minutes. The river was pretty big, but still, you made steady progress. I wouldn't say it was very long. But exciting. And you certainly needed the ferry, because there were no bridges in the area.

BAUMAN: Do you know how long your grandfather had been operating the ferry?

WIEHL: Oh, I think he ran that for, well, 20 years anyhow. Yeah, because he ran it right up until 1943, and certainly, from '23. That would have been 20 years. That much and probably more. Probably more. Probably back to maybe '13.

BAUMAN: That was probably operating up to 1943.

WIEHL: Oh, yeah. Right up to the time they left, and he took the keys with him. [*laughter*]

BAUMAN: So did you—your grandparents' ranch was on one side [the east side] of the Columbia from White Bluffs.

WIEHL: Mm-hm, was just across the river.

BAUMAN: Across the river. Did you go over there fairly often?

WIEHL: Oh, yes.

BAUMAN: And what sorts of things did you do?

WIEHL: I would be there when Grandpa would take the ferry over, and he'd maybe wait for 10 or 15 minutes or maybe sometimes longer. And if he had business—he was in charge, so he could pretty well decide when the ferry went back. And the ferry dock was right at the edge of town, and so I'd just walk up. There was a little landing. I'd walk up, and I'd be right in the center of town. The center of town—we're not talking a big town here. But there were stores there, and I was just—I'd go in and look around. And maybe sometimes I'd have a nickel or something like that, and I could buy something, generally sweet. And that would be a big, big deal. I picked a lot of potato bugs for a nickel.

BAUMAN: [*laughter*] Do you remember the names of any of the stores?

WIEHL: No, no. I remember a hardware store, though, that, in particular, that was just awesome, because it had things all over the walls, and it always sort of looked like a toy store as far as I was concerned. But it was clearly a hardware store.

BAUMAN: You mentioned earlier that at your grandparents' ranch, they often had sort of social events there. Do you remember any community or social events in White Bluffs, the town itself for like 4th of July or anything?

WIEHL: No. No, I don't. I don't remember anything like that. I do remember that my grandparents themselves had a couple of 4th of July—

BAUMAN: Okay.

WIEHL: —picnics or summer picnics. I don't know whether they were specifically 4th of July, when they would have friends and relatives in to share a lunch. And I can remember picnic tables being set out underneath the trees, and a lot of people being there. Everybody having a good time, and I remember that a couple of times. They were very sociable people. And of course, that was one way that people could get together with their neighbors and discuss the issues of the day, which were generally how to get better, get more income. And all the people in that area were really pioneers.

BAUMAN: Sure. Before we started talking, you showed me a photo of your grandfather in a baseball uniform.

WIEHL: Mm-hm. A White Bluffs baseball team.

BAUMAN: Right. I don't know, did your grandfather talk about that often? Do you remember your grandfather talking about that?

WIEHL: I have no memories personally of it, except that my father talked about the White Bluffs baseball team and was very proud of this picture of his father in uniform of the White Bluffs baseball team. Which was probably circa 1900 at that point. So clearly that baseball was very much a part of civilized life in the Hanford, Richland, White Bluffs area.

BAUMAN: Did you have any interactions with Native Americans in the area at all yourself?

WIEHL: I would see them. I myself had no interactions at that time. Later, I got to go onto the Priest Rapids reservation and was invited to one of the last—oh, they have a name for it—kind of a big celebration potluck that they had before they built the dam. But no, I didn't. I would see them, but I never had any contact. And the other thing, I wasn't afraid of them or anything like that. It was just that they weren't on my agenda for the day.

BAUMAN: How about neighbors? Were there—

WIEHL: There were virtually no neighbors. The ranch was it. My grandparents knew where their neighbors were, but they had to be a long way away. But they could ride and did ride over to wherever they were. I never saw a neighbor's ranch on our side of the river. So it must've been quite a distance.

BAUMAN: Right, right. And you mentioned you spent a lot of time playing with your aunt. Were there other children?

WIEHL: No. No, there were no neighbors. [*laughter*]

BAUMAN: Right. So you spent summers there up until 1943. So you and your family were living in Yakima when the government decided to build the Hanford Site.

WIEHL: Short notice.

BAUMAN: Short notice, yeah.

WIEHL: Very short notice.

BAUMAN: Do you have any memories of that, or stories that your parents have told you?

WIEHL: Oh, yeah. I have a memory, because I wasn't going there that summer. [*laughter*] And it was crisis time, because I'm guessing to a certain extent, but I won't be far off, that they were notified by telephone first and with a letter following. And they had something like 15 to 30 days—very short—in which that they had to get out. And this was the late winter of 1942 or the early part of 1943. Getting out is one thing, but where are you going to go? And so all heck broke loose. I mean, we've got to get out. Where are we going to go? And so the search was undertaken of where, because Grandpa was a rancher. He had all these cattle, horses. And so they eventually found a place near Selah, a ranch near Selah, which they bought. And they moved some of the livestock, which they did take with them. And he started anew in Selah and ran a dairy for probably about seven or eight years until after the war. When at that point, they had to move out. But they didn't have to accept the amount of money that the government gave them, and this was an important point. Some did, but those that didn't still had to move out. But after the war, they could take the government to court and prove that they did not get fair value for their land. And my grandparents did that. Of course, they had their own house attorney, my father. And they got probably in 1946 or 1947 fair value for the acreage that the government had taken. And with that, they then sold the ranch in Selah and bought a huge ranch up by Cle Elum in the Teanaway.

BAUMAN: Wow.

WIEHL: And moved there. Moved there, and lived—Grandpa lived a short but happy life in that area.

BAUMAN: Do you have any idea what the fair value was?

WIEHL: No. But it was substantially more than the government gave. The government wasn't interested in carving up nickels and dimes and half dollars. They wanted the land quickly. They got that, and then they would settle up accounts later. And it was a painful process if you were one of the people that got kicked off your land, but that's the way it worked.

BAUMAN: Yeah. I was wondering, do you remember or heard any stories or heard your grandpa or parents ever talking about their feelings about that, having had started this homestead and having been there for—

WIEHL: I think they looked at it—yes, I remember. And in particular, my uncle Elroy, who was pictured in some of those pictures that we were reviewing. He graduated from the University of Washington in 1941. And at that time, he was an ROTC cadet at the Reserve Officers Training program. He had been in that, and so he was going in to the Army in that summer. Well, that's perfect timing [*laughter*] for seeing a lot of action during the Second World War. And so he was an officer throughout the war, and, of course, was nowhere around in 1943. He was training for the invasion of Europe at that point in Fort Benning, Georgia, if I recall. And he never saw his—he left as a soldier, and at the end of the war, he couldn't go home. [*laughter*] I mean, his life had been uprooted. And that's just his personal case. And he was very matter of fact about it, but talked about it. It hurt him. But so what, really? I mean, we had to win the war. And I think that was the way my grandparents—I never—they wanted a fair price, because the government could do that, but they never argued or never felt badly about contributing to the quicker end of the war by the building of the atomic bomb. They felt pretty good about it, I think, that they had made a contribution. But then that doesn't entitle the government to steal it either.

BAUMAN: Sure, right. Let's talk a little bit more then about some of your family members. So you said your uncle Elroy was at University of Washington.

WIEHL: Mm-hm.

BAUMAN: Your father had already gone there.

WIEHL: Yes. He was a prosecuting attorney in Yakima at that time.

BAUMAN: And so you and your family were living there. And then your other uncle, Wright?

WIEHL: Yeah, he was the number one son, so he stayed with the ranch.

BAUMAN: Okay.

WIEHL: And so when they were kicked out of there in 1943, Wright went right along with my grandfather, went to Selah, and they bought a house for him right next door to or across the lane from where my grandparents were. And then when they went up to the Teanaway to Cle Elum, he went right along with them, and he was the foreman of everything.

BAUMAN: And then your aunt, obviously, would have been still young, so she—

WIEHL: Yeah, she graduated in late, 1950 or something like that from high school and married a man from Yakima.

BAUMAN: Are there any memories that stand out to you in terms of your times, your summers there that either are something humorous or just something that stands out particularly that we haven't talked about yet?

WIEHL: Well, I had a—well, I've told you that they had chickens. And so we ate a lot of chicken, and we had a lot of eggs. And my grandmother was very careful in selecting—we weren't going to eat a good layer. And so if the chicken was really performing out there with the eggs, then that chicken was safe for as long as that happened. [*laughter*] And of course, the chickens had to be killed.

Well, a lot of times, there was a chopping block out behind the house, and most of the time, my grandmother would go out there and chop the head off. And that was an awesome sight for a little kid, because she would chop the chicken's head off and plop the chicken down. The chicken would run around for a minute or so, until it finally flopped over, and then we had to pull the feathers and get the chicken ready to be put into a pot. Well, handy as my grandfather was, at one point, he went out there to do this trick— chopping the head off—and he took his thumb along with the chicken head. And so he picked his thumb up, and he was way ahead of his time on that, and cauterized the wound, and then drove all the way to Yakima, which was the closest major hospital where he could get aid. And that was a long drive in an old pickup, or new at that time. It was an awesome feat.

And he got there, and they said, no, we can't reattach the thumb. Which today they probably could do. Later that year, I had a friend in Yakima, and Grandpa would come up and visit us every once in a while. I had a friend, basically the same age, say, probably seven or eight, who sucked his thumb constantly. Little Ronnie, and he was always sucking his thumb. And Grandfather came out one day. We were playing out near the driveway where the car was. And Ronnie was sucking his thumb, and Grandpa says, you got to be careful about that, kid. You got to be careful. You shouldn't do that. And he says, I did, and look what happened, and he put up his hand, and there was no thumb, just a—Ronnie took his thumb out of his mouth, and I don't think he ever popped it back in again. That was it.

BAUMAN: Oh, wow.

WIEHL: That solved the problem. [*laughter*] So that was a—I was startled myself. [*laughter*] And that's one of the things that happened there that was kind of funny.

BAUMAN: Yeah. How would you, from your memories, describe your grandparents?

WIEHL: Very loyal, to start with, and very much involved in one another's lives, because they were in this together. A great feeling being around them. A great feeling. They were involved in everything together, and Grandmother was—Grandpa was smart. Grandmother was just as smart, and the two of them had physical constitutions. We had to be made of steel to live in there, and they were, emotionally and physically. That's a rare thing.

BAUMAN: Right. Yeah. Like to do what they did at the time they did is, owning that ranch and so forth, yeah. Did you see any other extended family much at all, either on your grandmother's side or your grandfather's [side]?

WIEHL: Oh, the extended—Wright was there, the oldest brother, because he was the chief hand. And he would be involved everyday on what needed to be done on the ranch. And one of the reasons my grandpa could slip away and run the ferry, because Wright was tending the ranch. He had a wife that lived there on the premises in another house. So that adds to the houses, which I forgot about.

BAUMAN: Oh, okay.

WIEHL: But they were always close at hand. And then he had a daughter. Wright had a daughter. He had a wife and a daughter, and the daughter then married, and her husband came on as a hand, too. So they had four or five other people that were in the mix all the time, all relatives.

BAUMAN: What was their last name, Wright's daughters and husbands?

WIEHL: Bobbi was her name, and I can't remember. Gaige. Yeah.

BAUMAN: Gaige, okay. I'm going to then go back and talk about your grandfather a little bit more. When we were talking earlier, I mentioned looking at census records. In 1940, he was the numerator of the census. I know he was very active in the community in addition to just being very busy with the ranch. Were there other positions, community positions that he held?

WIEHL: Well, he was the deputy sheriff in both counties, and that was important that it be in both counties, because you never knew which way the crooks were going to come, you see. [*laughter*] And he had a jail on either side of the river. And he had a photographic memory, which was the reason that he kept active those two jails, because they were all the wanted posters would come to him. They would go up on a bulletin board in the ferry boat or on the ferry boat. So if people were on the ferry, and there was nowhere to go. I mean, once you were on the ferry, you were stuck. You were like in a jail right then and there. If you were so unlucky as to be identified on the ferry, you would be escorted off at the other end to a local jail. And Grandpa picked up a lot of—I don't know a lot, but enough to talk about—of people going back and forth over the river there. So he was very much involved in that process.

BAUMAN: Were there ever any stories? Did he tell you any stories about any particular—

WIEHL: Well, I remember, this had nothing to do with the wanted posters, but it had to do with the jails. Since he was a deputy sheriff in both counties, occasionally, there might be a law enforcement issue. And generally, that involved people going across to White Bluffs, cowboys after a roundup, and having too much alcohol. Then the alcohol would take control of the situation. They'd get noisy, boisterous, maybe unruly, and when they got past the noisy area and into the unruly, then they would call for Grandpa. And that happened a couple of times, and one time, specifically, he went down there, and he would deputize people right on the spot. And they would take the drunken cowboys and throw them into the jail. Well, the one time they did that, two or three of them were thrown into jail, locked up, and Grandpa basically said, well, we'll see you in the morning and let you out then. Well, when he got there in the morning, the jail was gone. Somebody—his friends, these cowboy friends—the jail wasn't very big—they had lassoed the jail, pulled it off its little foundation that it was on, taken it 100 yards down the river and broken them out. [*laughter*] And he said, much to their credit, they came back sheepishly a few days later, helped move the jail back to where it was supposed to be, and repaired it so it was as good as new. [*laughter*] So the story had a happy ending, but I mean, that was kind of the justice of the Old West, I guess.

BAUMAN: Yeah. So was this jail in the town of White Bluffs itself?

WIEHL: Just on the edge. Closer to the river. He had it on both sides of the river.

BAUMAN: And then on the Franklin County side, was it right on the river too? Close to it?

WIEHL: Yeah. Both sides were very—more like a little outhouse.

BAUMAN: [*laughter*]

WIEHL: Which was susceptible to lassoing and moving, apparently.

BAUMAN: Yeah, right. It's that small. I think I know you were just there in the summers, so you didn't attend school—

WIEHL: No.

BAUMAN: —in White Bluffs. Churches—do you remember churches?

WIEHL: No.

BAUMAN: Did your grandparents go to church over there?

WIEHL: No, no, there probably was one. I'm sure there was one in White Bluffs.

BAUMAN: But you don't have any memories—

WIEHL: But I have no memory of going there, and I doubt if my grandparents did. They were probably still involved in the workday affairs of the ranch.

BAUMAN: Sure. And then I guess, any other memories that you have—you told some great stories. [*laughter*] Is there anything else that you remember from your summers there?

WIEHL: No, not specifically.

BAUMAN: And I guess the other question would be, obviously, the town of White Bluffs then in 1943 essentially ceased to exist.

WIEHL: Yeah, it did.

BAUMAN: That community. Why do you think it's important for us to remember the town, for future generations maybe to know about White Bluffs and the things that people like your grandparents did there?

WIEHL: Well, right now, it's forgotten. And that doesn't seem to be fair. A town should, once started, should live out its natural life. And this did not happen with White Bluffs. Its natural life was truncated suddenly by Presidential decree. And I think that an effort should be made to still let White Bluffs live out its natural life, and making a history of it may help. It may also help bring closure to a lot of the people that are now content that their story has been told. Here, living in Yakima, we tell our own story. We're there to tell our own story. But the people here didn't have that opportunity. So I think it's important.

BAUMAN: All right, well, thank you very much. I really appreciate you coming here and doing the interview—

WIEHL: My pleasure.

BAUMAN: —and telling the stories. They were terrific. Thank you.

Bibliography

HANFORD HISTORY PROJECT ORAL HISTORIES

Interviews conducted by Robert Bauman

Brinson, Robert. June 11, 2013.

Chalcraft, Lloyd. August 20, 2013.

Collins, Jack. August 4, 2013.

Dawson, Murrel. August 6, 2013.

Deranleau, Ray. September 3, 2013.

Finley, Catherine Borden. July 9, 2013.

Fletcher, Robert. August 20, 2013.

Gilles, Madeline. July 2, 2013.

Hansen, Edith. August 28, 2013.

Holm, Paula Bruggemann. August 6, 2014.

Johnson, Jean. July 31, 2013.

Johnson, Norman. November 5, 2013.

Kaas, Gordon. June 12, 2013.

Kleinknecht, Emma. June 12, 2013.

Reed, Leatris. August 27, 2013.

Sloppy, Laverne. July 22, 2014.

Sparre, Ilene Gans. August 28, 2013.

Wiehl, Dick. June 5, 2013.

Interview conducted by Laura Arata

Killian, Herman. March 3, 2014.

HANFORD CULTURAL RESOURCES LABORATORY (HCRL) ORAL HISTORY PROGRAM

Interviews by Robert Bauman

Brinson, Verna, and Louise McBride. August 28, 2000.

Buckman, Shirley. September 18, 2000.

Grisham, Walter. September 20, 2000.

Rawlins, Claude. October 1, 2000.

Interviews by Ellen Prendergast

Brinson, Verna, and Louise McBride. August 17, 2001.

Buckman, Shirley; Clarke, Alene, and Walter Grisham. August 6, 2001.

Bunnell, Rod. July 19, 2001.

King, Edith. August 20, 2002.

McGee, Yvonne and Dale. Telephone Interview. July 11, 2001.

Rawlins, Claude. July 24, 2001.

Slavens, Morris R. August 21, 2002.

Wiehl, Judge Lloyd. August 23, 2000.

BOOKS AND ARTICLES

Allen, John Eliot, Marjorie Burns, and Sam C. Sargent. *Cataclysms on the Columbia.* Portland, OR: Timber Press, 1986.

Armitage, Susan. *Shaping the Public Good: Women Making History in the Pacific Northwest.* Corvallis: Oregon State University Press, 2015.

Armitage, Susan, and Elizabeth Jameson, eds. *The Women's West.* Norman: University of Oklahoma Press, 1988.

Bauman, Robert. "Jim Crow in the Tri-Cities, 1943–1950." *Pacific Northwest Quarterly* 96, no. 3 (Summer 2005): 124–31.

Beardsley, Paul P. *The Long Road to Self-Government: The History of Richland, Washington 1943–1968.* Richland, WA: City of Richland, 1968.

Bechtel Hanford, Inc. *Phase II of the Pre-Hanford Agricultural Period: 1900–1943.* Department of Energy, 1999.

Brown, Donna. *Back to the Land: The Enduring Dream of Self-Sufficiency in Modern America.* Madison: University of Wisconsin Press, 2011.

Brown, Kate. *Dispatches from Dystopia: Histories of Places Not Yet Forgotten.* Chicago: University of Chicago Press, 2014.

———. *Plutopia: Nuclear Families, Atomic Cities, and the Great Soviet and American Plutonium Disasters.* New York: Oxford University Press, 2013.

Cannon, Brian Q. *Remaking the Agrarian Dream: New Deal Rural Resettlement in the Mountain West.* Albuquerque: University of New Mexico Press, 1996.

Carney, Todd Forsyth. "Utah and Mormon Migration in the Twentieth Century: 1890–1955." Master's thesis, Utah State University, 1992.

Carpenter, Stephanie Ann. "'Regular Farm Girl': The Women's Land Army in World War II." *Agricultural History* 71, no. 2 (Spring 1997): 162–85.

Chatters, James C. "History of Cultural Resources Management Activity on the Hanford Site," *Hanford Cultural Resources Management Plan,* PNL–6942. Richland, WA: Pacific Northwest Laboratory, 1989.

Coelho, Philip R. P., and Katherine H. Daigle. "The Effects of Development in Transportation on the Settlement of the Inland Empire." *Agricultural History* 56, no. 1 (January 1982): 22–36.

D'Antonio, Michael. *Atomic Harvest: Hanford and the Lethal Toll of America's Nuclear Arsenal.* New York: Crown, 1993.

Daubenmire, Rexford F. *Steppe Vegetation of Washington.* Technical Bulletin 62. Pullman, WA: Washington State University Experimental Station, 1970.

Fiege, Mark. *Irrigated Eden: The Making of an Agricultural Landscape in the American West.* Seattle: University of Washington Press, 1999.

Findlay, John M., and Bruce Hevly. *Atomic Frontier Days: Hanford and the American West.* Seattle: Center for the Study of the Pacific Northwest and University of Washington Press, 2011.

Freeman, Otis W. "Early Wagon Roads in the Inland Empire." *Pacific Northwest Quarterly* 45, no. 4 (October 1954): 125–30.

Freer, Brian. "Atomic Pioneers and Environmental Legacy at the Hanford Site." *The Canadian Review of Sociology* 31, no. 3 (August 1994): 305–24.

Gerber, Michele. *On the Home Front: The Cold War Legacy of the Hanford Nuclear Site.* Lincoln: University of Nebraska Press, 1992.

Glaser, Leah S. *Electrifying the Rural American West: Stories of Power, People and Place.* Lincoln: University of Nebraska Press, 2009.

Groves, Leslie R. *Now It Can Be Told: The Story of the Manhattan Project,* 2nd ed. New York: Da Capo Press, 1983.

Harris, Mary Powell. *Goodbye, White Bluffs.* Yakima, WA: Franklin Press, 1972.

Harvey, David W. *A History of the Hanford Site, 1943–1990.* Richland, WA: Pacific Northwest National Laboratory, 2000.

———. *Resource Protection Planning Process (RP3) Study Unit—Transportation* Olympia: Washington State Department of Community Development, Office of Archaeology and Historic Preservation, 1989

Hoelscher, Steven. "Review of Kate Brown, *Dispatches from Dystopia.*" *The Public Historian* 39, no. 1 (February 2017): 103–4.

Jameson, Elizabeth. "Toward a Multicultural History of Women in the Western United States." *Signs* 13, no. 4 (Summer 1988): 761–91.

Jeffrey, Julie Roy. "Narcissa Whitman: The Significance of a Missionary's Life." *Montana: The Magazine of Western History* 41, no. 2 (Spring 1991): 2–15.

Jensen, Joan M., and Darlis A. Miller. "The Gentle Tamers Revisited: New Approaches to the History of Women in the American West." *Pacific Historical Review* 49, no. 2 (May 1980): 173–213.

Johnson, Susan Lee. "'A Memory Sweet to Soldiers': The Significance of Gender in the History of the 'American West.'" *Western Historical Quarterly* 24, no. 4 (November 1993): 495–517.

Kirk, Ruth, and Carmela Alexander. *Exploring Washington's Past: A Road Guide to History.* Seattle: University of Washington Press, 1990.

Knobloch, Frieda. *The Culture of Wilderness: Agriculture as Colonization in the American West.* Chapel Hill: The University of North Carolina Press, 1996.

Kubik, Barbara. *Richland—Celebrating Its Heritage.* City of Richland, Washington, 1994.

Larson, T.A. "Women's Role in the American West." *Montana: The Magazine of Western History* 24, no. 3 (1974).

Lee, Erika. *The Making of Asian America: A History.* New York: Simon and Schuster, 2015.

Limerick, Patricia Nelson. *The Legacy of Conquest: The Unbroken Past of the American West.* New York: W. W. Norton, 1987.

———. "The Significance of Hanford in American History." In *Terra Pacifica: People and Place in the Northwest States and Western Canada,* edited by Paul Hirt, 52–70. Pullman: Washington State University Press, 1998.

Lyman, W.D. *History of the Yakima Valley, Washington, Vol. 1.* S. J. Clarke Publishing, 1919. archive.org/details/historyofyakimav01lyma.

MacDonnell, Lawrence J. *From Reclamation to Sustainability: Water, Agriculture, and the Environment in the American West.* Niwot, CO: University Press of Colorado, 1999.

Maloney, C. J. *Back to the Land: Arthurdale, FDR's New Deal, and the Costs of Economic Planning.* Hoboken, NJ: Wiley, 2011.

Meinig, Donald W. *The Great Columbia Plain: A Historical Geography, 1805–1910.* Seattle: University of Washington Press, 1968.

Mendenhall, Nancy. *Orchards of Eden: White Bluffs on the Columbia, 1907–1943.* Seattle: Far Eastern Press, 2006.

Moulton, Gary, ed. *The Journals of the Lewis and Clark Expedition.* 13 vols. Lincoln: University of Nebraska Press, 1983–2001. Volume 5.

Myers, Sandra. *Westering Women: The Frontier Experience, 1800–1915.* Albuquerque: University of New Mexico Press, 1982.

Neitzel, Duane Alan. *Hanford Site NEPA Characterization Report,* Rev. 17, PNNL–6415. Richland, WA: Pacific Northwest National Laboratory, 2005.

Nisbet, Jack, and Jack McMaster. *Sources of the River: Tracking David Thompson Across Western North America.* Seattle: Sasquatch Books, 1994.

Pacific Northwest National Laboratory. *The Hanford and White Bluffs Agricultural Landscape: Evaluation for Listing in the National Register of Historic Places.* September 2003.

Parker, Martha Berry. *Tales of Richland, White Bluffs & Hanford 1805–1943, Before the Atomic Reserve.* Fairfield, WA: Ye Galleon Press, 1979.

Peiss, Kathy. "'Vital Industry' and Women's Ventures: Conceptualizing Gender in Twentieth Century Business History." *The Business History Review* 72, no. 2 (1998): 218–41.

Powell, Lee Ann. "Culture, Cold War, Conservatism, and the End of the Atomic Age: Richland, Washington, 1943–1989." PhD diss., Washington State University, 2013.

Reid, Bill G. "Agrarian Opposition to Franklin K. Lane's Proposal for Soldier Settlement, 1918–1921." *Agricultural History* 41, no. 2 (1967): 167–80.

———. "Franklin K. Lane's Idea for Veterans' Colonization, 1918–1921." *Pacific Historical Review* 33, no. 4 (November 1964), 447–61.

Relander, Click. *Drummers and Dreamers*. Seattle: Pacific Northwest National Parks and Forests Association, 1986.

Rhodes, Richard. *The Making of the Atomic Bomb*. New York: Simon and Schuster, 1986.

Sanger, S.L. *Hanford and the Bomb: An Oral History of World War II*. Seattle: Living History Press, 1989.

———. *Working on the Bomb: An Oral History of World War II Hanford*. Portland, OR: Portland State University, Continuing Education Press, 1995.

Self, Robert. *American Babylon: Race and the Struggle for Postwar Oakland*. Princeton University Press, 2003.

Sharpe, James. *Pre-Hanford Agricultural History—1900–1943,* BHI–01326. Richland, WA: Bechtel Hanford Inc., 1999.

Smith, Sherry L. "Single Women Homesteaders: The Perplexing Case of Elinore Pruitt Stewart." *Western Historical Quarterly* 22, no. 2 (May 1991): 163.

Turner, Frederick Jackson. "The Significance of the Frontier in American History." *Annual Report of the American Historical Association, 1893*. Reprint, University Microfilms, 1966.

Webb, Walter Prescott. *The Great Plains*. Boston: Ginn and Company, 1931.

White, Richard. *"It's Your Misfortune and None of My Own": A New History of the American West*. Norman: University of Oklahoma Press, 1991.

———. "Race Relations in the American West." *American Quarterly* 38, no. 3 (1986), 396–416.

Worster, Donald. *Rivers of Empire: Water, Aridity and the Growth of the American West*. New York: Pantheon, 1985.

Contributors

Laura Arata is assistant professor of history at Oklahoma State University. A specialist in public history and the history of race and gender in the American West, her current book project, "Race and the Wild West: Sarah Bickford and the Construction of Historical Memory in Virginia City, Montana, 1870–1930," focuses on nineteenth and twentieth century Montana through the life of an African American woman. Dr. Arata received her PhD from Washington State University in 2014, and is the former co-principal investigator of the Hanford History Project.

Robert Bauman, volume editor, is associate professor of history at Washington State University Tri-Cities. A past director of the Hanford Oral History Project, he teaches American history and public history, including courses on the civil rights movement, immigration, migration and ethnic identity, and the Cold War. His research interests are in the areas of race and ethnicity in the American West and poverty and public policy. He is the author of the book *Race and the War on Poverty: From Watts to East L.A.* and numerous articles and reviews.

Robert Franklin, volume editor, is assistant director of the Hanford History Project and director of the Hanford Oral History Project. He holds a master's degree in history from Washington State University, where he serves as adjunct instructor. His teaching and research interests include twentieth-century U.S. history, history of science, historic preservation, and U.S. government planned communities in the Pacific Northwest and Alaska.

David W. Harvey, owner/principal of Northwest Cultural Resources Services in Richland, Washington, is a historic preservation specialist with expertise in preservation planning, cultural resources management, architectural history, and historic research in the Pacific Northwest, California, Alaska, and Montana. He managed and conducted the cultural resources mitigation and survey/inventory of the U.S. Army's Camp Hanford, located at the Hanford Site during the 1950s, and provided technical assistance for the rehabilitation of the historic White Bluffs Bank building.

Michael Mays, series editor, is director of the Hanford History Project and professor of English at Washington State University Tri-Cities. From 2012 to 2015 he was assistant vice chancellor for arts and sciences and then vice chancellor for academic affairs. Previously he served as department chair and professor of English at the University of Southern Mississippi. Mays holds a master's degree and PhD from the University of Washington and is author of *Nation States: The Cultures of Irish Nationalism* and numerous articles. He is a founding member of the Hanford History Partnership.

Index